THE REAL READ

Slightly Foxed

'A Hare's Breadth'

NO. 5 SPRING 2005

Publisher and co-editor Gail Pirkis
Co-editor Hazel Wood
Marketing Kathleen Smith
Publicity Stephanie Allen

Cover illustration by Linda Scott
An established illustrator, Linda Scott has enjoyed working for a variety of clients since graduating from the Royal College of Art in 1988. She also teaches at the London University of Arts and at Falmouth College of Arts. She can be reached on 07962 054647.

Original design by Octavius Murray
Layout by James Nunn

Colophon and tailpiece by David Eccles

Published by Slightly Foxed Limited
67 Dickinson Court
15 Brewhouse Yard
London EC1V 4JX

tel 020 7549 2121/2111
fax 0870 1991245
e-mail all@foxedquarterly.com
www.foxedquarterly.com

Annual subscription rates (4 issues)
UK £32; Europe £37; Rest of the World £42
Back issues are available on request.

ISBN 0-9548268-4-1

Printing and binding by Smith Settle, Otley

Contents

Contents

From the Editors

Slightly Foxed celebrates its first birthday this month, and we send special thanks and good wishes to our original subscribers who so sportingly took us on trust a year ago. We're absolutely delighted that so many of you have decided to re-subscribe – a good number for two years. If you know of anyone who just hasn't got round to it yet, it's still not too late, and our offer of a reduction on a two-year subscription still stands (if you're feeling generous, of course, you could always give them a gift subscription). And for anyone who missed the early issues and would like to complete the set, a limited number of back issues are still available.

On page 70, the audio producer Jonathan James-Moore describes the pleasure that Talking Books have given him, and we're pleased to be able to tell you that selections from *Slightly Foxed* are now available on tape or CD from National Talking Newspapers and Magazines (The National Recording Centre, Heathfield, East Sussex TN21 8DB; tel 01435 866102; e-mail info@tnauk.org.uk; website www.tnauk. org.uk).

Now spring is here, the season of literary festivals begins. Those of you who live in the Oxford area – and perhaps even those who don't but fancy a break in the city of dreaming spires – might like to know that we'll be appearing, with the novelist Penelope Lively, on 17 April at the Oxford Literary Festival to discuss the place of literary magazines and our experience of starting one. If the idea appeals, do please come along. It's always a pleasure to meet our subscribers in person, and – since we're new at this game – it would be soothing to our nerves to have you in the audience!

So *Slightly Foxed* has survived its first year, and we end it feeling optimistic. We've had a remarkable amount of friendly coverage in the press, from *Time Out* to the *Financial Times*, as well as on the web – an American website urges its readers to 'strike a blow for good reading everywhere and order a sample issue' (we already have a number of US subscribers, and if you have friends there who you feel might be interested we'd love to hear of them).

Above all, we've thoroughly enjoyed putting together something that seems to have given pleasure and relief to many and has brought us into contact with such an interesting group of people. We like to think of you, blocking out the horrors or boredom of planes and trains with the latest issue ('We seem to have done lots of flying over the past year – which I don't enjoy – and SF is just the job for sitting on a plane!'), falling asleep with it at night, wrestling it away from your spouse ('My wife and I quarrel over who should have it first!') or simply curling up with it in front of the fire for an indulgent half-hour – and we love the fact that you take the trouble to write or ring and tell us about it.

'I am completely enamoured of *Slightly Foxed*. It's like having a gorgeous new pet – lovable, fun and hugely intelligent,' was one of the accolades we enjoyed most – though looking at Jennings snoring loudly on his cushion, we did wonder about it a bit. But thank you for all your support and encouragement – and more happy reading in 2005.

GAIL PIRKIS
HAZEL WOOD

F.R. Leavis, by Mark Handley

A Hare's Breadth

PATRICK EVANS

'I hate 'em meself. They're too bloody stringy!' said the gamekeeper, holding up a pair of dead does. I leant out of the poacher's Range Rover and stroked one of their bellies. The doe was still warm, her tummy full of young and her teats ripe for suckling.

'Fiver each if you want one?'

We didn't.

'I'll give 'em to the lady vicar instead,' he said, tugging my sleeve conspiratorially. 'Big woman, likes her food. She has 'em jugged.' He sniggered.

This was my first real contact with hares. I had travelled with a hundred Cornishmen to a large Wiltshire farm bordering Stonehenge. The farmer invited us to catch as many live hares as we could for re-location to the South-West, where they are in decline. We caught the hares in long, low nets; their shrill screams rang out over the frozen flint-strewn fields, and three or four died from shock. The Cornish wanted them for sport, eventually, but they had immense respect for the animals. My own emotions about the catch were mixed, and I retreated from the cold February air wanting to find out all I could about the lithe, elusive, beautiful creature I had just met.

The librarian passed me a disintegrating copy of *The Leaping Hare*, by George Ewart Evans and David Thomson.

'Spring's the time to find out about hares,' she enthused. 'That's when you'll see them most, gallivanting on the new corn.'

George Ewart Evans and David Thomson, *The Leaping Hare* (1972)
Faber · Pb · 272pp · £9.99 · ISBN 0571106307

Reading the opening chapter, I was immediately sucked into a magical world. The hare's behaviour confounds science: it may move in a great drove like deer; it sucks milk from cows at pasture; it swims the Suir estuary in Ireland; it is intoxicated by snow, and makes tunnels in it for fun, despite not being a burrowing animal like its cousin the rabbit. And as part of an elaborate, little-understood mating ritual, it will sit transfixed in groups of thirty or forty, watching dancing, boxing males and females spar for attention.

In writing the book, the authors consulted the people who knew the hare best, those who saw it in the fields where they worked and hunted: farmers, gamekeepers and lurchermen. Yet these men's knowledge was not just based on experience, it was influenced by a mythological tradition dating back to primitive man. Cave drawings hint at this tradition and Celtic and Saxon practices confirm its transition into a relatively modern era. This includes the celebration of Easter, so named after the pagan goddess Iastre. Her primary talisman was the hare, and our Easter 'bunny' is just a corruption of the original image. The eggs we hide in the garden as children (or adults) were traditionally believed to have been laid by hares, a symbol of the forthcoming fertility of Spring.

At one time the hare was thought to be androgynous, just as a human embryo of either sex is initially identical. The hare also has a rare ability to conceive when already pregnant. Both its early and latter-day hunters believed it had the power to metamorphose into human form, and they celebrated this in totemic rituals, donning hares' ears and imitating its shrieks and leaps. The poacher with whom I travelled to Wiltshire wore a hat made of the head and forepaws of a young dog fox: a glance at him confirmed there was more to our relationship with hares than I had realized.

When George Ewart Evans and David Thomson began to collaborate on *The Leaping Hare* in the early 1970s, they had long been friends. Evans, the son of a Welsh shopkeeper, had for thirty years been working as a writer and oral historian. Thomson, a Scot, and also a writer, was a producer on the BBC's Third Programme. Each suffered from a disability. Evans was virtually deaf, and applied for a tape recorder. Thomson provided it, and together they subsequently made many programmes about rural life. Thomson himself was more or less blind; he gained an Oxford degree despite having all his books read to him by a female helper. But their greatest bond was a shared passion for stories first told in ancient times that had survived to the present day.

They divided the writing of *The Leaping Hare* chapter by chapter. Originally the book was Thomson's idea, but he was depressed and unable to tackle it alone: he had already spent two years working on his classic *Woodbrook*, and it would be another four before that was published. So he asked his old friend George for help, and after writing their respective parts, they swapped and edited each other's chapters.

Reading the book, I became fascinated with trying to decipher whose voice I was hearing. Both men were keen pursuers of a disappearing past: they loved to record the knowledge and folklore of people whose intimacy with the countryside was being swallowed up by mechanization. Evans's first book, *Ask the Fellows Who Cut the*

Hay, published in 1956, was the result of eight years' spent interviewing old people in the Suffolk village where he lived. Many of his sources of information about the hare and its behaviour came from people he got to know in this period. And their voices, like that of Percy Muttit, warrener and gamekeeper, call to those of us who have lived in the British countryside like the bells of a village church:

> I see a hare only last year come through the hedge when there was a chap a-rolling a piece o' corn; came through the hedge with a little leveret in her mouth on to the field and leave it.

Both men, too, owned the sometimes uneasy conscience of an educated mind that revelled in the value of the stories told by the poor and the socially repressed. For all that, *The Leaping Hare* has little political emphasis except for a wariness of an urban-dominated society. This, it argues, will diminish our understanding of the natural and supernatural forces that once coursed deeply through popular culture.

When it was first published, the book's use of oral history to explain British fauna came under attack from the senior academic establishment. But a younger, less entrenched readership (including Seamus Heaney) embraced the originality of *The Leaping Hare*'s arguments.

Opinions and insights from both scholars and country folk are layered successively, reflecting an oral tradition built on teaching that remained intact in the countryside for centuries. Direct quotations powerfully evoke conversations with gamekeepers and shepherds. We visualize them leaning on a gate, hands clasping the ash shaft of a fork or staff, looking out over the land they are describing and which they know so well. Through their voices the authors explore the dichotomy of our relationship with wildlife: the pleasure we derive from its beauty and vitality, and the sadness we experience in killing it for food or sport.

The book laments the increasing distance we feel from such animals in the modern world of supermarkets and 'managed' wilderness, and it also reminds us that it is stories that form the fabric of our existence, and that sustain us amidst a transient, evolving universe. It sees man and the hare as spiritual kin, and our relationship with this archetypal creature as emblematic of the ways in which we seek to fathom and control our natural surroundings.

For me, too, there was an additional pleasure in reading *The Leaping Hare*: it introduced me to the work of two often undervalued writers. Though they worked together, they were very different in character. David Gentleman, a close friend of both men and illustrator of some of their books, recalled:

> David [Thomson] was a real Scot, a heavy drinker; whenever he stayed with the Evanses, George would be obliged to come home early from the pub, because his wife was a devout Quaker. But David always stayed till closing time, and turned right out of the pub instead of left, and got a lift back with the police.

David's widow Martina Thomson described Evans to me as a man of 'proper' social behaviour, whereas her husband was altogether more emotional: 'You could see what he was feeling just walking around a room.'

Whenever I see a hare now, I think of what I feel for the countryside and its inhabitants, both human and animal, and I raise my hat and quote from the book: 'Good day to you, Sir Hare.' And I also think of the coincidences that united these men in their work, a union for which the reading public (and hares) should be grateful.

PATRICK EVANS spends a lot of time deciphering regional accents. He is currently writing his first book, about a Cornish boatyard.

Smoke Signals

JEREMY LEWIS

I am wretchedly ill-qualified to write about Simon Gray, since I am hopeless about going to the theatre and have never seen one of his plays. I plan to remedy matters as soon as I can, but in the meantime I cannot recommend his autobiographical writings too highly. *An Unnatural Pursuit* is, alas, out of print, but *Fat Chance, Enter a Fox* and the masterly *Smoking Diaries* have all been reissued in paperback, and only the most Cromwellian theatre-hater could fail to be touched, amused and thoroughly entertained by them.

Fat Chance and *Enter a Fox* are both very short, and follow a familiar pattern: Gray, fuelled by alcohol and fags, finishes a play, posts it off to various directors and producers, worries that none of them will like it, spends long lunches pondering their replies with his friend and neighbour Harold Pinter, agonizes about which actors should play particular parts, sips champagne during rehearsals, and is hugely relieved when the reviews aren't quite as bad as he'd dreaded. When not worrying about his play of the moment or pressing the wrong button on his computer – he wrote *Enter a Fox*, he tells us, to learn how to use the wretched machine – he talks to his dog George, and encourages him to strike up a friendship with a lonely fox which lives in his garden in Holland Park.

Those readers who like to learn as well as be entertained will

---

Simon Gray, *Fat Chance* (1995) · 126pp · ISBN 1862077460;
Enter a Fox: Further Adventures of a Paranoid (2001) · 122pp ·
ISBN 1862077452; *The Smoking Diaries* (2004) · 240pp · ISBN 1862077231
All £7.99 Granta paperbacks

discover a great deal about the workings of the British theatre: the rest of us can sit back and enjoy the prose of a writer who – like all the best playwrights, I imagine – has perfect timing and an impeccable ear. Nowhere is this more evident than in *Fat Chance*, and additional drama is provided by the fact that everything goes so disastrously wrong.

Gray had spent five years working on *Cell Mates*, a play about George Blake, who spied for the Russians, and Sean Bourke, the Irishman who helped him to escape from Wormwood Scrubs. Stephen Fry was eventually chosen to play Blake, and Rik Mayall was cast as Bourke, though Gray had never heard of either man before. Since the affable Fry was, like Gray, a product of public school and Cambridge, he seemed a kindred spirit, a 'puppyish enthusiast' who looked like a 'convivial prelate' and ended every conversation with 'God bless': Mayall was an unknown quantity and, on first acquaintance, less sympathetic. As readers may remember, Stephen Fry walked out of the production after two performances, and the stalwart Mayall was left to hold the fort. Fry, it seemed, had been unnerved by a review in the *Financial Times*, and thought he had let everyone down: despite fears that he might have committed suicide, he was spotted in the South of France wearing a beret, and was said to be contemplating a fresh start as a prep-school master.

Enter a Fox lacks the high drama of *Fat Chance*, but ample excitements are provided by the computer and by the nuts and bolts of getting *The Late Middle Classes* into production. We're also introduced to the heavily made-up figure of Mr Burn, a pederastic schoolmaster from Gray's prep school in Putney who resurfaces in *The Smoking Diaries*. Published last year, *The Smoking Diaries* differs from its predecessors in that it does not hinge on the production of a new play, and it interlaces explicit autobiography with scenes from the present day, many of which revolve around lunch with the Pinters and his partner Victoria Rothschild, the doings of his cats, and ruminative visits to the Queensway ice rink. Another difference is that Gray, who happily drained four bottles of Veuve Cliquot a day in his prime, has foresworn the booze in favour of Diet Coke, and is reduced to being a mere 'chain-smoking, teetotal, alcoholic wreck'.

Booze and fags loomed large in Gray's family. His brother and an aunt died of drink: his mother, a former Olympic athlete, refereed hockey matches with a cigarette in her mouth, and exclaimed on her deathbed, 'I'll tell you one thing, Si, I've learned my lesson! I'm never going to smoke another cigarette'; his father's cigarettes were confiscated as he lay dying, on the grounds that they were bad for his health. Gray Senior was a Scots-Canadian pathologist, and Simon Gray's early years were divided between Canada and South Kensington; he was, as a boy, a keen cricketer, playing for Westminster against Eton, and he recalls, with some nostalgia, the halcyon days when he dived into the Mediterranean with a cigarette clamped between his lips.

Written in a conversational, telegraphic style reminiscent of Molly Bloom and of Mr Jingle in *The Pickwick Papers*, *The Smoking Diaries* are opinionated, digressive and extremely funny. They're also very sad, as old friends like Ian Hamilton, another lunching companion, die of cancer, and Gray himself is threatened with the disease. As he contemplates, in moments of gloom, 'a life spinelessly lived, now supinely closing', he can draw some consolation from the immense pleasure the rest of us will draw from his version of events. I long to learn more; in the meantime, I must catch up on the plays.

JEREMY LEWIS's new biography, *Penguin Special: The Life and Times of Allen Lane*, will be published in May.

Tank Tracks

JULIET GARDINER

With its fashionable but unexplanatory one-word title, *Tank* is an easy book to overlook or misunderstand when you first come across it. Yet its jacket gives two clues as to why it is so absorbing, astonishing and enlightening.

The first is the name of its author, the cultural historian Patrick Wright, whose earlier books include *On Living in an Old Country*, *A Journey through Ruins* and *The Village that Died for England* – deeply satisfying studies of what appear to be recondite or small-scale subjects but which turn out to be profound excursions into the condition of England. The other is, in fact, its title: not *The Tank*, but *Tank*, which signals that this is no straightforward history but, in the author's own words, an appreciation 'that the poetics of the twentieth century extend far beyond the literary page' – extend indeed to the progress of this spellbinding piece of military hardware.

The tank is an emblem of state power, a behemoth that has transformed wars and threatened – and sometimes mown down – civilians. But it has also been seen as a 'cubist slug', has inspired a modernist song and dance routine *Tanko*, has led military men to philosophize, and installation artists to appropriate the rhomboid shape to suggest the ultimate in urban alienation. In short, the tank, as *Tank* so skilfully and wittily and sadly shows us, stands at the very heart of the twentieth century and points up its follies, its wickedness, its aspirations, its delusions – and occasionally its humanity.

Patrick Wright, *Tank: The Progress of a Monstrous War Machine* (2000)
Faber · Pb · 510pp · £12.99 · ISBN 0571207456

Although the tank had its origins in a 'modern steam chariot' – an invention of two Cornishmen in 1838 that would, as they put it, prove 'very destructive in case of war'– or even perhaps in Boudicca's chariot, in medieval suits of armour that were 'living tanks' or in Leonardo da Vinci's sketches, its moment was not to come until the First World War. Then the fortuitous arrival of three constituents – bullet-proof armour, the internal combustion engine and caterpillar tracks – enabled H. G. Wells's prophecy of 'Land Ironclads' to become reality. A lozenge-shaped machine of war, an 'armed caterpillar which could go through anything and knock down trees', would, it was hoped, bring to an end the slaughter on the Western Front.

It was there, in 1916, that the emblematic nature of the tank first became apparent. 'Gad,' wrote a battery sergeant-major of the 'Land Crabs', 'it struck me how symbolic of war they were, creeping along at about four miles an hour, taking all obstacles as they came, spluttering death with their guns, enfilading each trench as they came to it – and crushing beneath them our own dead and dying as they passed. Nothing stops these cars, trees bend and break, boulders are pressed into the earth.' Others spoke of tanks as 'low squatting things moving slowly in the mist' before heading back to their 'lair', while the restraints of censorship meant that war correspondents were obliged to compare these new armoured machines to 'giant toads, mammoths and prehistoric animals of all kinds'. Indeed, as Wright says, the tank triumphed as an exuberant metaphor long before it had been proved as a military machine.

The metaphor was continually reworked. In 1919 in the church of St Mary in Swaffham Prior, a small Cambridgeshire village, a stained-glass window was installed. Above the statutory biblical quotation, from the Second Book of Samuel – 'But the man that shall touch them must be ringed with iron' – was depicted a tank spraying fire over helpless British soldiers in an adjacent window. Two hundred and sixty-five First World War tanks that had been brought home more or less intact from France and Flanders served as giant piggy

Loading an early British Mark I tank (Imperial War Museum)

banks, sited in town and village squares to extend the idea of War Bonds and Certificates into peacetime thrift. But in Glasgow, the 'Haig' and the 'Beatty' – tanks that had raised over a million pounds – were joined in early 1919 by a 'tankodrome' in the city's Cattle Market, ready, if necessary, to quell the striking 'Red Clydesiders'.

Even so, in the period between the two World Wars, the tank's military advocates were few. 'Fighting the Germans is a joke compared to fighting the British,' one officer said in exasperation at an Army High Command that could not see the potential of mobile armoured weaponry, that persisted in treating the tank as if it were a Martello tower. One who could was Colonel J. F. C. 'Boney' Fuller, a Tank Corps veteran, whose interests lay in Eastern religion 'about which he could be bewildering', spiritualism, occultism, Shakespeare 'whom he admired and understood from an angle of his own', military history and the theory of war. His fascination with the occult drew him to the notorious Aleister Crowley; his belief that 'new ideas originate in piratical exploits outside the existing military organization' to Oswald Mosley and his British Union of Fascists.

When war came in 1939, Fuller, excluded from any position in the

Army, could only fulminate that while Britain's enemies had latched on to the potential of mechanized warfare, his own country's top brass was more concerned with rushing an additional two million men into the nation's army – 'human tank fodder', exploded Fuller – than with concentrating resources on what would win the war: 'tanks on the ground and aircraft in the air'.

Under the terms of the Treaty of Versailles, tanks had been forbidden to Germany, and at first German 'tanks' were but 'tactical representations' made of wood and painted canvas mounted on cars or tricycles. Hitler, however, was an aficionado of Fuller's theories, and in April 1939 he invited him to Germany, where he stood next to the Führer at his fiftieth birthday celebration and 'for some three hours watched a formidable mass of moving metal'.

'I hope you were pleased with your children?' Hitler asked.

'Your Excellency, they have grown up so fast that I now no longer recognize them,' replied Fuller.

It was these 'unrecognizable children' that swept through Poland four months later, a country with three and a half million horses and not a single factory producing cars. The brave but hopeless charge made by the Polish lancers against these great iron invaders became legendary. It was the same (or related) armour-plated 'children' that swept through the Netherlands, Belgium and France less than a year later, then Greece, Yugoslavia and the Western desert. It was tanks, too, that spearheaded the German invasion of Russia.

When the war was over – although in the twentieth century war was never over for long – some distant relative, a more honed and efficient reconciliation of the eternal contradictions of firepower, mobility and protection, permitted the small nation of Israel to 'win' in wars against her Arab neighbours. Some Israeli soldiers came to regard their tanks as home: 'You can be in a tank for days. You build them like a second home: pictures, a place to put your little packet of cigarettes, places to put your special tools.'

In the Cold War and beyond, the tank played a different role, allowing countries to use the might of state power against their own citizens or subject peoples. In Greece, during the Colonels' coup of April 1967, the CIA-backed Junta used tanks to kill hundreds of protesting students. In Chile, in September 1973, tanks in effect overturned the ballot boxes that had brought Allende to power. The same story was repeated in Budapest, in Warsaw and in Prague.

And it happened in Beijing in June 1989. But in Tiananmen Square a lone Chinese man stepped out in front of a line of tanks that had rolled down the Avenue of Eternal Peace after the massacre of protesting students. The leading '40-ton state war machine' veered to left and right: the young man veered with it. The tank stopped. The commander looked out. He and the young man spoke. When the 'mechanical ballet' was over, the young man cycled away. The tanks moved on. The tank commander was demoted for 'the worldwide shame he had brought on the People's Liberation Army' by stopping. But the young man was hailed in the West as democracy's hero.

In the early hours of 28 April 1991, a Soviet T-34 tank that had stood for fifty years in a square in Prague as a memorial to Soviet soldiers was painted shocking pink by David Cerny, a student at the city's Academy of Applied Arts, and some fellow-students who styled themselves 'The Neostunners'. When the outraged government had the tank rendered drab again, fifteen Czech parliamentary deputies dressed in blue boiler suits, with an initial on their backs to indicate that they were deputies and were therefore immune from prosecution, painted the tank pink again. Alexander Dubçek was obliged to take a plane to Moscow to apologize to the Soviet authorities.

That same year, the year of 'Desert Storm' – the perfect textbook war as far as the US military was concerned – Krzystof Wodiczko, a Polish artist living in New York, constructed a tank to 'defend' the homeless who had been betrayed and then harried by the city's first black mayor, the Democrat David Dinkins. The 'Poliscar', a flimsy, electronically wired, wigwam-like structure, was described as 'a war toy for the homeless' and 'a robot with a tank-shaped body geared for

survival in a police state' by the art critic of the *Village Voice* after she
had been to see it in a Manhattan gallery.

Meanwhile, as the century turned, further south at Fort Knox,
top military thinkers were planning 'the war after the next one' with
the aid of cyberspace. In a simulated world of virtual reality, eager
tank soldiers picked up the art of 'terrain visualization', familiarizing
themselves with the landscape of a distant country so that, when they
invaded, they would know it better than the local population. The
revolution in technology now meant that the tank could penetrate
the fog of war while still maintaining its essential shock element.
Perfect lethality – the ability to destroy the enemy without incurring
casualties of one's own – now seemed possible.

But the Cold War was over. Even before 9/11, before the war in
Iraq, those concerned with the development of military hardware
had recognized that while 'a large dragon had been slain', we now
live in a jungle filled with 'a bewildering variety of poisonous snakes'.
Who knows what role the tank will play in this new landscape?

Tank is a far from dispassionate account. Patrick Wright has followed the tank's tracks and then made connections, visited places,
talked to people and out of this spun a powerful, individualistic
narrative that is both a history of our times and a lesson for the
future. Its erudition, elegance, irony and sense of foreboding make
it essential reading. 'Don't be too painstaking in putting in every
rivet,' *Tanks and How to Draw Them*, published in 1945, advised.
'Leave something to the imagination and try to develop the art of
suggestion.' Here the rivets are all in place, but Wright does not, for a
moment, fail to suggest the meanings and portents that can be drawn
from the progress of this 'monstrous war machine'.

JULIET GARDINER has been writing about various aspects of the Second World
War for over a decade but she still only ventures with trepidation into the fringes
of that territory claimed by military historians. Her latest book, *Wartime: Britain
1939-1945*, was published last year.

Cooking for Love

KATHARINE DAVIES

There must have been a thousand books in the sitting-room by the end, each a doorway leading somewhere I had never been before. And even after I had read all of them, each time I looked I would find something new. A play of light and shadow; something flitting in and out of a story I knew by heart.

Each time I read *Reef* – the story of a boy, Triton, growing up as a servant and cook in Sri Lanka in the late 1960s – I find something new. I think the way that *The Tempest* flits in and out of the novel is one of the things that keeps me rereading it. Another is the play of light and shadow in Romesh Gunesekera's prose.

I lived in Colombo from 1992 to 1994, teaching English, and my first home was on Havelock Road where, only the year before, a bomb had exploded, throwing severed heads and body parts into the air. This, by Sri Lankan standards, was nothing. Like many others, I was struck by the incongruity of such horror in a country so deceptively gentle, one that looked so much like the Garden of Eden. In *Reef* Gunesekera seduces you with a charming depiction of a lost era, but underlying it all is the knowledge of the killing that came later.

The novel is framed in the early 1990s but recalls, through the eyes of a boy on the brink of adulthood, a period when the island was on the verge of its first insurgencies. Triton, its narrator, and his

Romesh Gunesekera, *Reef* (1994)

Granta Books · Pb · 192pp · £6.99 · ISBN 1862070946

master, Mister Salgado, eventually flee Sri Lanka for a new life in London after the 'disappearance' of Mister Salgado's closest friend. So it is from England, after twenty years of 'staggering brutality' in Sri Lanka, that Triton looks back on their life there; an encounter with a Tamil refugee in a petrol station takes him back to 'a bay-fronted house six thousand miles away'.

When I first read *Reef*, I was taken back all those miles too. I felt a surge of joyful familiarity with the scarlet-flowering *rathmal* and the jasmine, the 'reddish clay curls' of the roof tiles, the crows, the fish and the fishermen, and the hawkers who come singing down Mister Salgado's lane. I re-tasted the sweetness of pineapple jam and the fieriness of *seeni sambol*. I recognized the furniture and the polished floors of the house, and the rhythms of Sri Lankan voices. I remembered a hot Christmas of my own.

Actually, the Sri Lanka of the 1960s was as distant to me, in 1992, as the old cook Lucy-*amma*'s past was to Triton – 'She had seen monkey suits give way to Nehru shirts; Sheffield silver replaced by coconut spoons.' But because everything is explored through the eyes of a young servant, attentive to the smallest of domestic details, this gives a very intimate picture. And I admit that, somehow, Mister Salgado's house merged in my imagination with another house down another lane that I had known, a house that it could almost have been.

I have never read a more haunting re-imagining of *The Tempest* than *Reef*. Gunesekera plucks certain ingredients from the play and stirs them into the story as deftly as Triton/Ariel whips up his delicacies in the kitchen. Mister Salgado makes a wonderful Prospero. He's 'a real gentleman', a marine biologist, an expert on the fast-disappearing coral reef, who smells of cinnamon bushes and has a voice so 'captivating' that it enables Triton to see the whole of their world: 'the great tanks, the sea, the forests, the stars . . .' The *Tempest* allusions ebb and flow throughout, giving the whole book a touch of magic.

Triton is 11 and still believes in magic when he comes to work for Mister Salgado. He has been brought by an uncle after accidentally setting fire to one of the huts of his rural school and has been told to do 'whatever the hell he tells you'. At first the house is the centre of Triton's universe – 'Even the sun seemed to rise out of the garage and sleep behind the del tree at night.' But Mister Salgado is Triton's teacher as much as his master. Triton falls under his spell and he watches him 'unendingly'. Mister Salgado makes lists while listening to *The Mikado*, and Triton copies him and learns to write. He watches Mister Salgado reading, feeling 'the air move when he turned a page, each one catching the lemony light, slice by papery slice'. Likewise, Triton also reads alone, 'unfettered', swept up in other worlds, forgetting where one story ends and another begins, the 'only sound the sound of onion-skin rustling from story to story'.

In 1992, all I saw of Sri Lanka was the richness and strangeness of everyday life in a tropical paradise. My view, like Triton's, was a narrow one that only gradually widened. Only later was I fully aware of the bloodbath, 'hidden from the eyes of the world' by 'the sun and the wind and the dirty blue sky'. One day, Triton recounts for Mister Salgado the *Anguli-maala* story of the prince who was punished by being made to collect a thousand bleeding fingers and turn them into a garland. Each time he threaded on a new one, ten old ones fell off. He could not stop killing. 'Down on the beach, the bodies of men and boys who had disappeared from their homes . . . slaughtered by him . . . were washed in by the tide.' If anything can come close to conveying the tragedy of Sri Lanka, it is this macabre allegory, as told by Triton.

In Triton's own sphere, he learns that 'what has happened *has* happened', that it 'hangs on the robes of the soul'. When he looks at Mister Salgado he realizes that it 'takes time, years, to learn how other people cope with themselves, how they come to terms with the changes that happen, always happen around them'. The parallel with Sri Lanka itself makes this very moving. A decade on, with the long ceasefire said to be under threat, *Reef* has lost none of its resonance. It is a book about change, about shifting boundaries, about what happens when things are lost or destroyed and about how people carry on in whatever way they can.

It is a love story too. Exquisitely pretty, but thoroughly modern, Miss Nili (who works at the Sea Hopper Hotel) interrupts Triton's own love for Mister Salgado when she comes to tea and turns their world upside down. Poignantly, it is Triton who seduces her for Mister Salgado with the richest, juiciest 'love cake' ever made. Mister Salgado watches her in awe, unable to eat a crumb. 'He makes a lovely cake,' says Miss Nili, endearing herself to Triton for the rest of his life. Triton learns to be a marvellous cook, and he learns about love, discovering that food and love are strangely intertwined. By the end of the novel, he understands at last who he really is, and finds his own place in the world.

The descriptions of food in *Reef* are so delicious that I cannot resist giving you Triton's recipe for an egg flip – a 'mixture of high-grown coffee, cocoa, raw egg, vanilla and brandy whisked with hot milk and butter and stirred with a cinnamon stick; sprinkled with ground nutmeg'. But the magnificent Christmas dinner Triton cooks up at the heart of the book, during which so much changes for all the characters, I will leave you to discover and relish for yourself.

KATHARINE DAVIES's first novel, *A Good Voyage* (published this year in paperback as *The Madness of Love*), is inspired by *Twelfth Night* and is set partly in Sri Lanka. She now teaches Creative Writing, although she once spent a slightly foxed five months working in the offices of a certain quarterly.

Ex Libris IV

SIMON BRETT

In Europe, bookplates are not just pasted into books but are commissioned and collected as a form of miniature graphic art in their own right. Under Soviet rule they also became a means of asserting individuality and national identity and of sustaining foreign contacts, under the noses but beneath the interest of the authorities. Classic, academic training was abandoned over a century ago in the West, but artists in the countries of the former Soviet Union and its satellites live with the result of that tradition having been retained. Classical figures, symbols and gestures are still familiar to them and they have the fluent craft and drawing skills to match. Some divert the language into surrealist modes, but many use it straightforwardly, and without irony.

The work of the Estonian artist Lembit Lôhmus is finely crafted to a degree most Western engravers are scarcely capable of. At a simple level it excites simple admiration. But inasmuch as its visual language carries resonances we have virtually forgotten how to use, it can also remind us, rather bracingly, of the limitations of our own outlook.

Lembit Lôhmus, Graniidi 16-12, Tallinn, EE-10413, Estonia; e-mail: lime@hot.ee

Horn-rims and Baggy Chords

ARIANE BANKES

In George Ramsden's quiet secondhand bookshop, Stone Trough
Books, in York, he normally has a publishing job on the go as well.
Editing (letters of Siegfried Sassoon at the moment) and book-design
absorb him to the extent that he may barely notice when a customer
comes in. Indeed, with his horn-rimmed spectacles under a shock
of rigid hair, and a manner combining chivalry with extreme vagueness, he has the air of a startled hedgehog when spotted beyond
the bookstacks. His series of catalogues – a leisurely fifteen spread
over twenty years – are typographically understated, without colour
illustration and with only scant recommendation of the books, but
nevertheless beautifully designed, as are his own publications. He
confesses to being a complete amateur as regards design but his life
has become infused with the subject, and he now ponders title-pages,
wine-labels, logos on lorries, sheet-music covers, even shop fascias,
with an unusual degree of discernment.

I first met George when he was running his shop at the bottom of
Camberwell Grove in south London, the target of many a Saturday
expedition in the 1980s. It was rather a long haul from Islington,
and spirits would sometimes flag as we crawled in a tailback along
the Walworth Road, only to pick up again at the sight of Camberwell
Green and the thought of Stone Trough just round the corner. Not
that we ever received an effusive welcome from the diffident George

---

Stone Trough Books, 38 Fossgate, York YO1 9TF

tel 01904 670323 • fax 01944 768465 • e-mail george@stonetrough.demon.co.uk

– but somehow we felt, deep down, that he probably was rather pleased to see us. Indeed if we timed our visit around lunchtime he might lock up the shop and meet us halfway, in the ramshackle basement of a vast and gloomy antiques shop, where we would lunch on Irish stew and a bottle or two of red wine, while business presumably languished back at the ranch – Saturday must, after all, have been his busiest day.

Stone Trough Books was a small two-roomed shop but somehow it stocked everything you had ever wanted to read, and lots of books you didn't realize you wanted to read until you saw them there, lined up in their faded dust-jackets, their titles and authors inviting you in. They were marshalled in a way that led you on from one author to another through friendships, influence and association. You could browse for hours, and often did, coming away with a small hoard of voices to keep you going until the next visit: it seemed so stupid while you were there not to buy a hardback of Vita Sackville-West's garden book to replace your dog-eared paperback, and a couple of Iris Origos. George, who had served three years' apprenticeship at Heywood Hill's bookshop in Mayfair without imbibing any of the positive sales pitch practised there, always looked faintly surprised that you wanted to buy anything at all, and seemed loath to take your money, but if you persevered you could build up quite a library for yourself. To this day, the casual browser at Stone Trough need have no fear of being browbeaten into buying anything: as George himself puts it, 'Some booksellers are persuasive recommenders – it's a huge gift. I find it very difficult to sell books verbally. Things tend to go better if I walk away from the customer.'

The atmosphere was quiet but friendly, more like a house than a shop. If it was very quiet and there was no need to keep an eye on things downstairs, George would say, 'Why don't you come upstairs and see Edith?' Then you would be led up to a lovely room lined from floor to ceiling with Edith Wharton's library, recently purchased from Maggs. It contained some 2,000 volumes but was incomplete, and it was George's mission for many years to fill the gaps, tracking down volumes from far and wide that contained her bookplate or inscription, and restoring them to their rightful position. (In 1999, mission accomplished, he was to publish the complete catalogue of Edith Wharton's Library, with an introduction by Wharton's biographer Hermione Lee.)

When not hunting down books or selling them, George founded and played trombone in a rollicking jazz band called Baggy Chords, much in demand at parties. George's vagueness was legendary, however. Once, after a particularly lively gig, he reported sorrowfully to the exhausted members of the band that he could not ferry them and their equipment home, as his car had been stolen from the road outside. He had overlooked the fact that he had recently traded in his old vehicle for a less dilapidated model, which was all the while sitting exactly where he had parked it.

Many were the cries and lamentations when George shut up shop in Camberwell Grove to migrate to York, but within weeks he had found premises at 38 Fossgate, in the heart of York's second-hand book world, and within months he was fully installed in a space which looked remarkably like the last, though there was no room for Edith – she was moved to the house where the family now live. Part of the gravitational pull to Yorkshire was the proximity of Rupert Hart-Davis, living in a congenial haze of pipe-smoke and anecdotes in the Old Rectory at Marske-in-Swaledale amidst his library of 17,000 books and his collection of pictures. Old rectories could be said to be the leitmotif of George's life: he himself lives in one, which resembles in some respects those of Reynolds Stone at Litton Cheney and of Rupert Hart-Davis: books everywhere, various publishing projects simmering away in different rooms, the lingering trail of wood smoke, paintings and prints on every wall.

Stone Trough's catalogues have specialized in the libraries and collections of distinguished bibliophiles: A. J. A. Symons (1991), John Gere, and the writer-and-photographer partnership of Olive

Cook and Edwin Smith (2003) among them. But it was Hart-Davis who provided the catalyst for the first book under the Stone Trough imprint when he invited George to publish a collection of his tributes to writers, *Praise from the Past*. There followed an edition of Christopher Isherwood's early letters, bought at auction, and in 1997 the bibliography of Christopher Logue, an altogether more extravagant production, with colour tip-ins of his poster-poems. By this time George Ramsden had met George Mackie, the inspired former designer at Edinburgh University Press, whose influence can be seen in this and subsequent Stone Trough publications.

Stone Trough Books is almost a one-man band: George does the typesetting and design which is fine-tuned by the printer/binder Smith Settle (the printer, incidentally, of this quarterly), in addition to the usual publisher's tasks of arranging printing and distribution. The very pleasing results are available on-line and by mail order from George himself. He can publish exactly what he wants to, when he wants to, and is beholden to no one; he keeps his initial print runs small but has been known to reprint titles such as *George Lyttelton's Commonplace Book*. The list is as idiosyncratic as its publisher, pursuing the byways rather than the highways of literary life.

Bensoniana and Cornishiana is one of his more wilfully eccentric publications, soon to be reissued with a dashing new dust-jacket by Mark Hearld, whose design for Timothy d'Arch Smith's memoir of managing the Times Bookshop in the 1960s propelled it off the shelves at such a rate that it is now out of print. *Bensoniana* comes sparkling from the notebooks of A. C. Benson. *Cornishiana* collects together the often baffling and unwittingly droll remarks of Blanche Warre-Cornish (1844–1922), the wife of an Eton beak, an apparent paragon of respectability given to making the sort of pronouncements that stopped people dead in their tracks in that less enlightened age. 'Tell me,' she asked a young lady, 'whom would you rather have had for a lover, Shelley, Keats, or Byron? I'd give all three of them for one wild half-hour with Rossetti.' She was fond of dispensing advice:

to a friend who had just arrived (uncomfortably) on the shores of southern Africa, she wrote an encouraging letter: 'In all disagreeable circumstances remember the three things which I always say to myself:

"I am an Englishwoman."

"I was born in wedlock."

"I am on dry land."'

Another of my favourite titles is *The Bronze Horseman* (1999), a translation by Robert Powell-Jones of a handful of Pushkin's finest poems together with his novella 'The Shot'. Powell-Jones, whose early death exemplified Cyril Connolly's dictum 'Who the gods wish to destroy they first call promising', provided a witty and illuminating introduction, and John Bayley a foreword. One learns a great deal about the irrepressible and unimaginably gifted poet from this slim volume (in his youth, egged on by his friends, he would extemporize verse lying flat on his back on the billiard table of his club), and if you ignore Powell-Jones's entreaty at the end of the Introduction to 'learn Russian. It is not a difficult language, you could pick it up in months, and you would be spared the translations', you will read here his remarkably successful versions of some of Pushkin's lesser known works.

Work in progress at Stone Trough (when not manhandling quantities of books, sorting, pricing and shelving, bent double over boxes), now revolves around editing and annotating letters written in the last ten years of his life by Siegfried Sassoon to Mother Margaret Mary of the Convent of the Assumption, his confidante in all things spiritual and quotidian. These will make their appearance in two volumes over the next two years, and then, who knows? But whatever appears between the covers will be unusual, enlivening, and beautiful to behold and to hold; of that you can be certain.

ARIANE BANKS works as a publisher and editor, and can never resist buying three books for every two she reads.

Drama in Suburbia

ADÈLE GERAS

Ever since he drew my attention some years ago to the best book I've read in the last decade – *Time Will Darken It* by William Maxwell – I have trusted Nicholas Lezard's judgement. And if I remember correctly, it was his recommendation in the *Guardian* that also made me rush out to find *Revolutionary Road* by Richard Yates, of whom I had never heard. It wasn't in the shops, so I had to order it.

When the book arrived, I was almost put off by the image on the jacket. It was of a car, and if there's one thing guaranteed to make me not want to pick a book up, it's a machine on the front. (There's a lively debate among the writers I know about what constitutes an effective cover. I say a human face or figure is a good idea. A friend of mine who writes romantic comedies disagrees: what she likes is a landscape or a still life. Some say blue is a turn-on, others hate books with brown covers.)

Ignoring the car, however, I turned to the accolades on the jacket. David Hare, Kurt Vonnegut and even Tennessee Williams had apparently all adored it, and the introduction was written by one of my favourite writers, Richard Ford. I read the book at once and ever since I've been trying to tell people about it without, I fear, making much of an impression, except on members of my own family. My

Richard Yates, *Revolutionary Road* (1961)
Methuen · Pb · 346pp · £7.99 · ISBN 0413757102
A new biography of Richard Yates has also just been published.
Blake Bailey, *A Tragic Honesty: The Life and Work of Richard Yates* (2004)
Methuen · Hb · 708pp · £24 · ISBN 0413774325

husband became such a fan that he then went on to buy and read Yates's other (excellent) novels.

Revolutionary Road was first published in the United States in 1961 where it was nominated for a National Book Award and was very successful. It didn't, however, do very well when it was first published in this country in 1986. So what can I say to persuade readers of *Slightly Foxed* that here is something out of the ordinary and well worth searching out? Well, paradoxically what makes it extraordinary is that it's about unremarkable people who live in ordinary houses in an ordinary street in suburban America in the Fifties. Realist fiction at its very best tells us not only about its characters but also about ourselves, and there are so many emotions here that we can all recognize, so many situations that we can understand. To read *Revolutionary Road* is to inhabit Yates's suburban world.

Frank and April Wheeler have two children and they live in the Revolutionary Road of the title. He is a small-time ad man and she has dreams of something better than her present life. She's a member of the local amateur dramatic society and the novel begins with the toe-curling embarrassment of her first-night failure. You could say that the action in the rest of the novel stems from that night. Eventually April decides that if the family uproots itself and moves to Paris, then all will be well. Frank and she will both fulfil their potential abroad in a way they never could at home.

You know, as the reader, that it will end in tears, and so it does. The family never does get to France. Frank has an affair at the office. April becomes pregnant by another man. And their lives unravel before your very eyes. Their neighbours, their friends, the whole community, in fact everything around them, conspires to confound their dreams. The plot has an inevitability and inexorability reminiscent of Hardy, but I won't give away any more of it here.

The best thing about Yates's work is not so much what he does as the way that he does it. His writing is so good that you don't notice how he achieves his effects: it's never arty or self-conscious but seems, in the words of Joseph O'Connor writing about John McGahern, 'as if it had somehow grown on the page'.

Here he describes the Wheelers' feelings as a row evolves into something ghastly:

> Then the fight went out of control. It quivered their arms and legs and wrenched their faces into shapes of hatred, it urged them harder and deeper into each other's weakest points, showing them cunning ways round each other's strongholds and quick chances to switch tactics, feint, and strike again. In the space of a gasp for breath, it sent their memories racing back over the years for old weapons to rip the scabs off old wounds; it went on and on.

But Frank and April love one another and the tragedy is that all their love and shared life aren't proof against the ambushes of circumstance. Yates is wonderful at pointing up the gap between our fantasies of what we could be and what we truly are: flawed creatures who have to do the best we can whatever happens to us. Although it has touches of humour, *Revolutionary Road* can't be called a happy book. But reading it leaves you in awe of a writer who has gazed unflinchingly at his characters, understanding them completely and revealing their secrets to his readers.

So ignore the car on the cover and read this great novel. It is one that you won't forget.

ADÈLE GERAS has written more than eighty books for children and young adults. Her first novel for adults, *Facing the Light*, was published in 2003 and her second, *Hester's Story*, this January. She lives in Manchester.

Daughters of Time

ROGER HUDSON

Outbursts of memoir-writing by women followed both the English Civil Wars and the years 1789 to 1830 in France, the period encompassing the Revolution, Napoleon, the Restoration and the July Revolution. It is hardly surprising since both these were periods of profound upheaval, when events left a deep impress on people's minds as well as a desire to explain and justify them, and their own behaviour at the time, to future generations. Mrs Lucy Hutchinson, Ann, Lady Fanshawe, Margaret, Duchess of Newcastle and Anne, Lady Halkett were followed 150 years later by Mesdames de Boigne, de La Tour du Pin and de Rémusat. The reissue of Madame de Boigne's book in translation drew me back to reread the last three.

Adèle de Boigne was the youngest of this trio, born in 1781. Her father, the Marquis d'Osmond, an officer in Louis XVI's army and then a diplomat, was from an old and distinguished aristocratic family. Her mother, one of the thirteen children of Robert Dillon, an Irish Roman Catholic man of business settled in Bordeaux, was lady-in-waiting to Madame Adélaïde, one of Louis XV's daughters. Her memoirs pass swiftly over the first decade of her life and she recalls only isolated incidents: asking Louis XVI for two drops from a chandelier when she knew her ears were going to be pierced; her tears freezing on her face as she and her family, now exiled by the French Revolution, crossed the Alps on mules to save money.

Memoirs of the Comtesse de Boigne (2004)
Helen Marx Books, distributed in the UK by Turnaround · Pb · 2 vols.
304pp and 256pp · £9.99 each · ISBNs 1885586639 and 1885586736

After two years in England, their finances in desperate straits, Adèle took matters in hand by marrying a self-made Savoyard soldier of fortune, General Benoît Leborgne (later the Comte de Boigne), in London in 1798. She was 16 and he was 49, and she told him to his face that she did not care for him in the least. He had amassed great wealth in the service of the Mahratta princes in India – soon to be subdued by Sir Arthur Wellesley.

Madame de Boigne's father, an enlightened man with time on his hands, had overseen her studies, 'and my English education also turned me instinctively in the direction which has since been called liberal'. She qualifies this, however, by saying she could 'only conceive of liberty, apart from licence, as based upon a strong aristocracy'. She admitted that she felt the attraction of Napoleon, but she detested his tyranny when she saw it in operation in the years following her return to France from exile in 1804. Yet she had the gravest reservations about the Bourbon princes: the Comte d'Artois (later Charles X) and his sons and, to a lesser extent, the Comte de Provence (later Louis XVIII), surrounded as they were by ultra-reactionary royalist émigrés. In the well-worn phrase, they had learnt nothing and forgotten nothing, and failed to see, as she clearly did, that the *ancien régime* was gone for ever.

Madame de Boigne and her family were financially independent thanks to her by-now-estranged husband's riches. They bided their time until Louis XVIII was restored in 1814, when her father took up his diplomatic career once more, first as ambassador in Turin and then in London. Madame de Boigne went with him, remarking on the silence of the London crowds, on 'the yellow cloud which seems like a vast extinguisher placed over the city', and on the immense routs when carriages were regularly smashed in the crush to deposit guests.

After a few years her father became disenchanted with the increasingly reactionary direction in which France was heading and so retired, which enabled Madame de Boigne to return to Paris and set up a salon, one of the most select and distinguished among those that adorned the capital during the Restoration: 'My invitations were verbal and were supposed to be given by chance. I was, however, careful to see that chance should bring my way those persons whom I wished to have meet one another.'

Her salon provided her with a grandstand from which to view the obtuse blunderings of the older branch of the Bourbons during their last decade of power, and the positioning of the younger Orléans branch so that they could seize their opportunity when it came. Through her we experience the assassination of Artois's son at the Opera in 1820; the announcement of Napoleon's death on St Helena, producing 'no more effect in the street than the advertisement for a lost dog'; the Duchesse de Montmorency's vow of chastity and how it ended; the Queen of Sweden's infatuation with the king's first minister; and the diseased imagination of Tsar Alexander of Russia, who thought everyone was laughing at him.

Once the 'mulishly obstinate' Charles X came to the throne in 1824, in his late sixties, it was not long before attention was focused on his son. 'Alas not the glimmer of the sound sense on which France had set her hopes for many years was to be found in him . . . It was this circumstance which . . . exasperated all minds and drove both parties to excesses.'

In July 1830, when Paris finally took to the streets, Madame de Boigne knew something was up when 'none of the workmen employed at my house had come back since dinner time'. The fatuity of the Ultras surrounding the king contrasted with the high level of organization among the insurgents, led by the students of the Polytechnique. Madame de Boigne claimed to be nothing more than 'a fly on the coach wheel' but in fact took an active part, particularly since her lover Etienne-Denis Pasquier was a major political figure. Anxious to ensure that the Duc d'Orléans became Louis-Philippe, King of the French, she carried messages and arranged meetings, as well as attempting to get the histrionic and self-regarding Chateaubriand on board.

Madame de Boigne's memoirs end with this, for her, supremely successful outcome. She was on terms of the greatest intimacy with the new royal family, and soon they would make her commoner lover both Chancellor of France and a duke. For someone whose outlook, though sharply intelligent, penetrating and clear-sighted, remained thoroughly aristocratic, this was all highly gratifying. Denied by the first Revolution that position at the centre of things that would otherwise have been her birthright, she had got there in the end, however circuitous the route.

*

The *de haut en bas* tone of Madame de Boigne is the true voice of Versailles and the *ancien régime*, and its somewhat disdainful superiority is to be treasured by anyone trying to understand it today. It is a tone that can also be detected, though not nearly so insistently, in the memoirs of the Marquise de La Tour du Pin. She was born Henrietta-Lucy Dillon in 1770, the daughter of Arthur Dillon, commander of the Dillon Regiment in the French army, and brother of the 12th Viscount Dillon. Her mother was a lady-in-waiting to Queen Marie Antoinette. The Dillons were Irish in origin and had raised a regiment for James II in 1688, which then formed part of the Irish Brigade, in the service of France until 1794 when its remains passed into the pay of Britain.

Apparently there was little love lost between Mesdames de Boigne and de La Tour, and one suspects that at the bottom of this there lay the latter's denial of there being any blood relationship between her father's family and Madame de Boigne's relations, the Dillons of Bordeaux. In spite of this Madame de La Tour's great-uncle, another Arthur Dillon who was the Archbishop of Narbonne, did much to further the careers of the Bordeaux Dillons. But that in itself was a second reason for her hostility, since the Archbishop had in effect defrauded her of a large part of her inheritance.

A further cause of friction may have been that Madame de La

Tour's husband succeeded Madame de Boigne's father as Minister to The Hague, but unlike him he actually took up residence there in 1791, undeterred by the civil unrest in Holland. Then Madame de Boigne had married a *parvenu*. Lastly, Madame de La Tour lost both her father and her father-in-law to the guillotine in 1794, and came close to losing her own head too, while Madame de Boigne's family had already been safe abroad for some years. A sneaking suspicion arises that Madame de Boigne played the aristocratic card as often as she did because she felt undermined by her mother's ancestry and her husband's origins.

Madame de La Tour's memoirs end in 1815 and the most interesting passages deal with her life during the years of the Revolution, during her exile in America from 1794 to 1796, and from 1808 to 1815 when her husband was one of Napoleon's Prefects in Brussels, then Amiens. Her mother died young, while her father was away fighting the British in the American War of Independence or governing French colonies like St Kitts. She was brought up by a domineering and ruthless grandmother and was always under threat of being dispatched to a nunnery if she crossed her. She gives us arresting vignettes of the *ancien régime*. Dancing, for example, was unpopular when she was very young because of the constrictions of the fashions of the time:

> narrow heels, three inches high . . . a pannier of stiff, heavy whalebone spreading out on either side, hair dressed at least a foot high, sprinkled with a pound of powder and pomade which the slightest movement shook down on the shoulders, and crowned by a bonnet known as a pouf on which feathers, flowers and diamonds were piled pell-mell.

Looking back she has only contempt for the childishness of her life at court, 'laughing and dancing our way to the precipice'. She remembers the uncouthness of the short-sighted Louis XVI, 'like some peasant shambling along behind his plough', while Marie Antoinette had 'great courage but little intelligence, absolutely no tact and worst of all, a mistrust of those most willing to serve her'. She recalls the almost convulsive way the queen used her fan at the opening of the States General, the event which signalled the beginning of the Revolution. She and her husband were in the thick of the terrifying episode at Versailles in October 1789 when the mob arrived to take the king and queen back to Paris.

The march of the market-women on Versailles

As the situation became increasingly threatening in Paris after the execution of the king in January 1793, she and her husband left for their château near Bordeaux, but they were soon forced into hiding when the Terror spread there. Her description of those days recalls nothing so much as the lives lived by the Resistance during the Nazi occupation – with hideouts, safe houses, couriers, rationing and forged papers. In one house in Bordeaux where she took refuge she could hear the roll of drums every time the guillotine fell in the Place Dauphine.

With the help of steadfast friends they managed to escape on an American ship in 1794. There followed something of a rustic idyll, farming 250 acres in Albany, up the Hudson River, growing maize, making cider and butter with the help of their slaves, observed by the local Shakers and Red Indians. One day Talleyrand, that figure of quintessential sophistication, but then also in exile, arrived to find her, chopper in hand, preparing a leg of mutton for the oven.

The de La Tours returned to France in 1796 to reclaim their château within the time limit set by the government. They went with great reluctance, since 'France had left me only memories of horror'. The following year they fled yet again after the suppression of a royalist conspiracy put the lives of aristocrats at risk once more. England was their refuge, where they stayed with relations in East Anglia and then in a tiny house in Richmond, at one point down to their last £5. Once Napoleon's seizure of power had finally settled France, they came back to the château and scratched a living for the next eight years by distilling grapes from the surrounding vineyards into brandy.

Their fortunes turned when Napoleon and his wife Josephine came through Bordeaux on their way to Spain in 1808. Madame de La Tour's stepmother was a first cousin of the Empress and this was enough to secure a summons to wait on the imperial party. Almost immediately the Marquis found himself appointed Prefect of Brussels with the brief of winning over the local aristocracy, something which he and his wife were almost too successful in achieving. In 1813 Napoleon removed him from his post after malicious reports that people went to their house in Brussels as if to a court. His wife's immediate reaction was to go to see Napoleon at Versailles. At the end of an hour's audience, 'He spoke these amazing words, "I was wrong. But what can be done about it?" It was perhaps the only time in his life that he made such an admission . . . "There is Amiens. Would that suit you?" "Perfectly, Sir," I replied without hesitation.'

They were not to be at Amiens for long because Napoleon's star was fast waning. When she was visiting Paris in 1814 Talleyrand came to see her:

Attempts to arm oneself against his immorality, his conduct, his way of life, against all the faults attributed to him were in vain. His charm always penetrated the armour and left one like a bird fascinated by a serpent's gaze . . . Taking a candle from the table, he began to study the engravings hanging in fine frames around the walls of the room: 'Ah, Charles II, James II, just so' . . . 'Heavens,' I cried, 'what is all this talk of Charles II and James II? You have seen the Emperor. How is he? What is he doing? What does he say after a defeat?' 'Oh, don't talk to me about your Emperor. He's finished . . . And now, away with you . . . Give Gouvernet [her husband] my good wishes. I am sending him this news for lunch. You will arrive in time.'

Although the Marquis de La Tour had grave reservations about whether the Bourbons had learnt their lesson, he went on to serve them as Minister at The Hague again, then as Ambassador in Turin. After July 1830 he and his family even continued to support the claim of Charles X's grandson, the Duc de Bordeaux, and this meant they ended their days in exile from France yet again.

*

Madame de Rémusat came from a legal family, and her husband too was a lawyer. This in no way prevented them from suffering during the Revolution: he lost his job as a magistrate while she lost her father and grandfather to the guillotine. This was not the only thing she had in common with Madame de La Tour. It was thanks to a connection with Napoleon's wife Josephine (a friend of Madame de Rémusat's mother) that this 'little person, ordinary looking, cold and reserved, in nowise remarkable, devoted to the duties of a pure and virtuous life', as she described herself, became one of her ladies-in-waiting in 1802, while her husband became Prefect of the Palace and later Chamberlain to the Emperor. Her aim in writing her memoirs was to describe 'how she at first loved and admired, next condemned and dreaded, afterwards suspected and hated, and finally renounced' the Emperor. In fact her book ends in 1808, some time before she took that final step.

She mounts a devastating indictment. Looking back, she admits that, in 1802, 'to rely on the hopes that Napoleon inspired was, no doubt, to deceive ourselves, but we did so in common with almost all France'. While still First Consul, Napoleon introduced regal elements into his everyday life, much in the manner of President Putin in recent times. But the event which first made her 'blush in secret at the chains I wore' was Napoleon's kidnapping and killing of the Duc d'Enghien, a royal prince, in 1804. On the night before Enghien was shot she heard Napoleon say, 'Bloodletting is one of the remedies of political medicine. I stand for the state, I am the French Revolution.'

Once he had declared himself Emperor later that year, but had refused to give a constitution to the French, whom 'he regarded as fickle children ready to be amused by a new plaything', he had to 'conciliate and fascinate them by every possible means'. The 'fatal lure of military glory' was one of these and 'a fever of etiquette' at Court, that 'living puppet show set up to surround the Emperor with what seemed to him necessary state', another.

She felt Napoleon spread disquiet and distrust on purpose. 'Where he could not perceive vice, he sought for weakness or, in default of this, he carefully inspired fear, so that he might always be the stronger.' She accused him of a 'supreme and universal contempt for human nature', and, more specifically, of a dislike of all his Marshals. 'Who has not heard him say that he preferred men of second-rate abilities?' At Court, 'In every ceremonial he was too precipitate . . . and neither knew how to put people at their ease nor cared to do so, for he avoided the slightest appearance of familiarity.'

This broad characterization of the man is supported by details that fill out the picture:

He regularly ruined his footwear by poking the logs in the fire with them; he taught himself to shave for fear of having his throat cut; he refused to repeat himself when dictating, which he always did at great speed; he was abstemious except for coffee; he took great care of his hands and nails, and got through sixty bottles of eau de Cologne a month.

As well as giving one of the most perceptive portraits of Napoleon, Madame de Rémusat's memoirs are a mine of information on the rest of the Bonaparte family, on the Empress and her increasingly troubled relations with her husband, and on her own unlikely friendship with Talleyrand. The acuteness of her analysis of him – as a man disgusted with his own cold-heartedness who 'has long been blasé on every point, and seeks for excitement as a fastidious palate seeks for pungent food' – tells us exactly why he enjoyed her company. The moderate line he advocated fell on deaf imperial ears, but it chimed with her own feeling that Napoleon was constantly 'diminishing his attention to the welfare of France', which he saw as 'only one large province of that empire he was striving to bring under his rule'.

It is a regret that Britain did not produce similar memoirs by women from these years, but also a reflection of the fact that her period of real upheaval was behind her. From it had emerged constitutional arrangements strong enough to withstand the assaults of Napoleon and to absorb the demands for reform which followed in 1830, a year in which, as Macaulay pointed out, she was able to 'afford an ignominious shelter to the exiled heir of forty kings' – Charles X.

ROGER HUDSON has worked in publishing all his life and latterly has compiled a number of books for the Folio Society including *The Grand Quarrel*, selections from the Civil War memoirs mentioned in paragraph one.

The last English edition of the *Memoirs of Madame de La Tour du Pin* was published by Harvill in 1999. The *Memoirs of Madame de Rémusat* are harder to find: the last time they appear to have been reissued is 1895.

Admirin' Byron

RANJIT BOLT

That a romantic could have also been
So classical is striking you'll agree
Though waxing passionate when we are green
And cooler when mature is probably
A change determined in the very gene
Or so at any rate it seems to me –
Our grasp of life is just that bit more firm,
Our reason turns like the proverbial worm.

And in *Don Juan* it turns like billy-oh.
(*Don Ju-an* is the poem's actual title
But it would cause the line to overflow
Its metric banks so, scansion being vital,
I plumped for *Juan* just then; for all I know
I shall again, though not to scan it right'll
I fear annoy you, and you doubtless yelped
At this misnomer, but it can't be helped.)

I read it first when I was seventeen
And it enthralled me even then despite
My being obviously far more keen
Than comprehending; long into the night
I'd labour over what a line might mean

Lord Byron, *Don Juan* (1821)

Penguin · Pb · 760pp · £15.99 · ISBN 0140424520

And sometimes wish, though fairly erudite,
He hadn't put in such a host of quotes
My nose was all but buried in the notes.

At thirty I returned to it with glee,
Its wit, its charm, its wisdom and its wry,
World-weary take on life delighted me.
Civilization is distinguished by
Such understatement and such irony,
And they're what make the English, by the by,
(Or so, for all he hated them, thought Byron)
A race one simply cannot help admirin'.

To quote a poem in a poem seems
A touch like fraudulently expediting
One's composition; when one's own rhyme scheme's
The same as that about which one is writing
The fraudulence is worse; so, though my theme's
A literary critique, I shan't be citing
My subject; you must take it from the shelf
And look for illustrations for yourself.

What's that I hear you say? You haven't got it?
Off to your local bookshop, then, at once!
Not got *Don Juan*? You should be garrotted!
And when there's so much sawdust in your bonce,
As every reader's brain these days is dotted
With books to which the only right response
Is to forget them all as soon as read,
A feat that's sometimes harder done than said.

If his prosodic geyser tends to gush
In later cantos, and his scansion slackens,

The early ones (don't take them at a rush
But mull and ponder them) in which he blackens
Hypocrisy and lies and cant and mush –
A modern Jason taking on those krakens
Quite fearlessly – display a touch so light
It makes one wonder why one tries to write.

Some critics claim the poem's core and pith
Lie in the figure handed down to us
By Molière, Molina, Mozart, myth,
Pace those pundits, I don't see it thus:
Byron had enemies to tangle with
And many burning issues to discuss
And chose the libertine dragged down to Hell
Where other heroes would have done as well;

Don Juan's the poem's spokes and not its hub
Or else its hub when that bit matters less
Than do the spokes; a part but not the nub;
The manikin but not the actual dress;
Or, in bridge parlance, not a lesser club
But not a high spade either; if success
(To get back off this metaphoric limb)
Depended on him, yet it wasn't him.

Byron is what this poem is about
If about anything, that is, per se,
And if he'd sought a different subject out
From here to Timbuktu, now till doomsday
I, for my own part, seriously doubt
If he'd have found a better. Anyway
He will repay you, whether dipped into
Or, novel-fashion, simply read straight through.

Wordsworth, among the verse he slams is yours,
For me, at least, one of his noblest aims,
Since I'd consign without the least remorse
Most if not all your poems to the flames
Along with Coleridge's (bar two, of course)
While Keats, with great percipience, he names
As promising, though he cannot excuse
His sensitivity to bad reviews.

The bards he loves are Milton, Dryden, Pope,
And there again, of course, he doesn't err,
Seeing how superior in technique and scope
To his contemporaries those poets were,
Historically he seems to interlope
Among his own peers, never their confrère
But championing the measured and the sane
In an epoch with fever of the brain.

When he does wax romantic for a while
In Canto Two, where Juan's ship is wrecked
And he hooks up with Haidée on her isle,
It's brought off to such dazzling effect,
So sweetly do both verse and tale beguile
The reader's ear and heart and intellect –
The whole thing somehow viewed askance yet felt –
How could the staunchest cynic fail to melt?

The book is seldom serious for a minute
But sometimes is for two or even three,
By which I mean that there are stanzas in it
Where Byron is, or leastways seems to be,
Pronouncing from the heart. But three's his limit
And even then he will immediately,

As if it wasn't really him that spoke,
Explode his own intention with a joke.

This, and its harsher, more acerbic traits,
Are what should make this poem, for my money,
Compulsory reading in these dreary days
When being frank, fearless, sometimes even funny
Is almost frowned upon, and what one says
Right down to whether it is wet or sunny
Must undergo self-censorship until
It can be grasped by any imbecile

And guaranteed to cause no toss-wit pain . . .
My thousand words are up. I have to go.
You'll read *Don Juan* if you've got a brain,
You'll need much more than that to grasp it though –
To pin this Proteus down's a long-held aim –
I thought I had for a half a sec, but no –
Perhaps I shall before I bite the dust –
Till then you'll have to take my praise on trust.

––––––––––

RANJIT BOLT's a translator for the stage
And specializes in French plays in rhyme.
He had a job once with a steady wage
But gave it up in 1989
When his Corneilles were briefly all the rage.
Original work comprises at this time
One novel, *Losing It*, now pulped and gone
But still available from Amazon.

An Island Apart

MILES HORDERN

When I left university I spent six months before the mast, working on a yacht crossing the Pacific. Except this was in 1988 and times had changed. With two small children on the boat, my role was that of both deckhand and nanny. As the ketch fell off a wave and Barbie's head became detached from her neck for the second time that watch, I longed for gales so that I might be called urgently on deck.

The children's mother had, in a former life, been an editor, and the ketch was equipped with that item as essential on sailing boats as sails: a good library. Gales turned out to be less frequent at sea than they are in books so I pulled a battered hardback from the shelf and started to read. A European man arrives on a tiny Pacific island and sets about making a home. The story was superficially similar to other accounts from the early 1900s: Arthur Grimble in the Gilbert Islands, Tom Harrisson in the New Hebrides. But *We the Tikopia*, by the New Zealand-born anthropologist Raymond Firth, turned out to be something else again.

Tikopia is an island apart. It lies 1,500 miles east of Australia in that part of the Pacific known as Melanesia. But culturally Tikopia's population is Polynesian. For reasons that are not entirely clear the Tikopia 'back-migrated' from the Polynesian heartlands in Samoa and Tonga, sailing west against the general flow of migration about a thousand years ago. Today the island is technically part of the Solomons, but it is largely autonomous. Its inhabitants, whose skin

Raymond Firth, *We the Tikopia* (1936)
Routledge · Hb · 664pp · £75 · ISBN 0415330203

is the colour of copper, are quite alone in a black-skinned Melanesian sea. It is this combination of isolation and insularity that has made Tikopia a favourite subject for anthropologists.

After reading Firth's book I longed to visit the island, but this same isolation made such a possibility seem unlikely. Eventually, however, in July 2003, I anchored my 28-foot sloop in a bight in Tikopia's fringing reef. On the beach I was mobbed. The islanders hoisted my canoe on to their shoulders and, singing and chanting, carried it up the sand in accordance with Polynesian custom. Beneath the casuarinas I found the site of the house where Raymond Firth had lived in the 1920s, and nearby stood the house of Ariki Tafua, the chief of the district. My sloop's anchor was sunk in Ariki Tafua's lagoon and I owed him tribute.

I crawled on hands and knees through the doorway of his house. Inside, three elderly women, their chins and chests tattooed, were smoking pipes. Ariki Tafua lay sprawled on his side. Firth described the incumbent chief in the 1920s as a 'strong willed old man with an eye for the main chance'. His great-grandson had clearly inherited the same characteristics. He showed little enthusiasm for the gift I had brought. Instead, he told me he had a severe headache, a boil and a sore knee. Did I have any aspirin on the boat? I brought him half a dozen Codeine and a brace of Valium. After that Ariki Tafua was always pleased to see me.

Certainly, there have been some changes on the island since Firth's day. The men have swapped their bark-cloth girdles for shorts and T-shirts; only the older women go bare-breasted. And since the island converted to Christianity in 1956, tattooing has become rare among the younger generation – in Firth's day most adults had full body and face tattoos.

But in many other respects it is remarkable how little has changed. There is still no shop, airstrip, wharf or phone, and a ship calls only every four to six months. The method of constructing the grass houses has also barely changed. The lozenge-shaped roofs are low-slung, the sago thatch eaves touching the sand, to withstand the destructive cyclones that threaten the region every year.

The lives of the islanders are also still governed by the daily imperative of procuring food. With a guide I climbed to Te Uru o te Fenua – the Head of the Land – a 1,000-foot peak on the crater rim at the island's centre. From here it was clear that the island was a monstrously impractical place for human beings to live. Its total land area is less than three square miles and much of that is precipitous. The Tikopia literally swarm all over their blue-bordered rock, digging gardens in which to grow taro or yams on any ledge where soil has formed. From the summit I occasionally caught sight of them, stick figures glued to the emerald volcano's outer flanks with breakers foaming on the reef beneath their heels.

The task of feeding the population occupies the Tikopia every day and often through the night. Riches are only described in terms of food. A wealthy man is *tanata kai kai lasi* – a man who eats greatly. After ten centuries of scratching the barest of livings from this volcanic pile, the Tikopia have learnt that it will support a population of 1,200 and no more. In the past, therefore, nature was ruthlessly controlled. Only eldest sons were permitted to marry. Others were free to take as many lovers as they liked, but any progeny were killed. Firth recalls how one chief, in the course of a famine, took his young sons out to sea in a canoe so as not to be a burden on precious food supplies. An ancient song of Tikopia refers to drowning at sea as 'sweet burial'.

The surrounding ocean is an ever-present force. The massive posts which support the houses against ocean storms are whole tree trunks, the roots buried in the ground, just as a ship's mast is stepped below the deck. The posts divide each house into two parts: inland/profane; seaward/sacred. The terms 'inland' and 'seaward' are used for all sorts of spatial references on the island. Firth was once with a group of men working in the gardens when one said to another, 'Friend, there is a spot of mud on your seaward cheek.'

In *We the Tikopia* the islanders prefix almost every statement with 'friend', especially when they are addressing Firth himself. I must admit, I was suspicious when I read this. Europeans in the South Pacific have been all too inclined to impose their own imagery. Arthur Grimble in the Gilbert Islands (today's Kiribati) translated the Gilbertese language as a form of quaint Olde English: 'Thou comest . . .'; 'Behold!' But I was wrong. In the five days I spent on Tikopia I was never once called by name, only 'friend' or 'brother'.

Firth came to Tikopia to study kinship. He found that, ultimately, the island operates as one interdependent kinship group. The title of his book is itself a phrase that was constantly on the islanders' lips: an individual would reply on behalf of the entire population, 'We the Tikopia believe that.' The features one might expect to find in a work of anthropology are of course present in the book: social structure, ceremonial traditions, pagan beliefs, building methods, crops, prehistory. But it is Firth's account of the people themselves that makes his work unique. The island characters he introduces are the antithesis of Robinson Crusoe's compliant slave Man Friday. Firth's Tikopia are bitchy, proud, passionate, confident and clever. It takes him months of painstaking diplomacy to win their trust, but when he has done so they hide nothing from him and he diligently records it all: marriages, affairs, elopements, love triangles, modes of sexual gratification, lechery, lewd behaviour and feuds.

He also provides characterization and dialogue to flesh out his examples. Indeed, his supporting evidence is so detailed and fulsome it is surely more than is strictly necessary in the name of academic enquiry. But then that is the great beauty of the book. In cool, dry prose Firth relates how the islanders curse and make love, dance and die, dress their hair and smother their unwanted children.

The result is a rounded and complete insight into the workings of a pre-literate culture. Firth captures the sometimes suffocating intensity created by 1,200 people living cheek-by-jowl on an ocean-girt precipice where the only means of escape is death. He records several incidents of suicide, particularly among those disappointed in love, usually achieved by swimming alone out to sea.

The tensions that are sometimes apparent among the Tikopia are understandable. But their labyrinthine code of taboos can be baffling. This is never more the case than in the story Firth tells regarding Pu Sao, a commoner who made the mistake of breaking wind in the presence of several chiefs and other men of rank. Pu Sao was so overcome with shame that he climbed a nearby coconut tree to escape the humiliation. His lifeless body was found in the crown of the tree several days later. He had committed suicide by 'impaling himself through the fundament on one of the hard dry spathes, sharply pointed, which are usually to be found there.'

We the Tikopia has sometimes been compared to the novels of Dickens or Eliot because it captures the whole gamut of life. But perhaps a better comparison would be with *Moby-Dick*, Herman Melville's portrait of life aboard a whaler. Just as in *Moby-Dick*, in *We the Tikopia* the reader enters a self-contained world bounded by the ocean, one that is at once familiar and alien, claustrophobic and vital, fascinating and appalling.

Raymond Firth was professor of anthropology at the London School of Economics from 1944 to 1968. He returned to Tikopia many times and wrote a total of ten books about the island. The last, *Tikopia Songs*, was published in 1990, when he was 90 years old. The island today is one of the most comprehensively documented societies in the ethnographic record. When Firth died in 2002 his official obituary described him as the father of modern British anthropology. To mark his death Routledge have reissued a limited edition of *We the Tikopia*. In view of its price, I don't imagine you will rush out to buy a copy, but I do urge you to borrow one, if you can, from that much underrated institution, the public library.

MILES HORDERN mostly sails alone, accompanied only by a good library. His book of voyages to Tikopia and beyond will be published this year.

The View from Denestornya

RUTH PAVEY

Count Miklos Banffy's *Transylvanian Trilogy* is a long novel about the follies, beauties and shortcomings of Hungarian society in the decade leading up to the First World War. He wrote it during the 1930s, when the disastrous outcomes of that war were still developing. Nostalgia may have been an active ingredient of this project, but Banffy's purpose was to record rather than gild what had been lost. One of his conscious motivations was to help future Hungarians understand their past.

Since he was not writing for a twenty-first-century English-speaking audience, we may perhaps be forgiven some haziness about facts he takes for granted and which colour everything he writes – for instance, that Hungary was on the losing side in the First World War; and that before the Empire which it uncomfortably shared with Austria fell apart, Hungary was about three times its current size. Transylvania, the setting of much of the narrative, was then under Hungarian rule, although most of its people were ethnic Romanians.

The titles of the three volumes, borrowed from the fiery words written on Belshazzar's palace wall, give immediate warning that this is a story of loss: *They Were Counted, They Were Found Wanting, They Were*

Miklos Banffy, *The Writing on the Wall: The Transylvanian Trilogy* · Translated by Patrick Thursfield and Katalin Banffy-Jelen; *They Were Counted* (1934) · 596pp · £12.99 · ISBN 190085015X; *They Were Found Wanting* (1937) · 470pp · £12.99 · ISBN 190085029X; *They Were Divided* (1940) · 326pp · £11.99 · ISBN 1900850516 · All Arcadia paperbacks

Divided. The trilogy was a success when it first came out, but since its viewpoint is aristocratic it sank from view during the Communist era and has only recently resurfaced. I came across it when the first volume appeared in English and the others were still being translated. Very far as my family ever was from castles in Transylvania or grand balls in Budapest, something in the tone of the writing, the buoyant voice tinged with wistfulness, drew me in. It is a voice from just before 1914, an era which has special resonance for me.

My father was the third of seven children of a Somerset parson. According to his sister, he was already seen as 'a bit difficult' before he sailed off to Gallipoli as a very young officer. He was wounded, but recovered enough to carry on. Or so it seemed, till he had a breakdown in the 1920s. As far as I know, little that happened to him during the rest of his life made him feel comfortable, except marrying my mother, but she died too early. I remember him as an elderly man, gallant but often mournful, with an aura of nostalgia around him that was all the more powerful because he spoke so little, either of the past, or of what he was feeling.

Miklos Banffy, by contrast, is a man who *wants* to talk. Not about the war – he, being older than my father, did not have to serve in it – but about the world it hastened away. In some respects, the fact that he is recalling rural Transylvania rather than Somerset makes little difference: it is still the same era, when life in the countryside, though no one yet knew it, was about to change; cars and machinery were appearing, the men and the horses would soon be sent to war, the outworn stability of relationships between people of different classes could not hold. By contrast with England, however, the middle classes in Transylvania were only just getting into their stride, and a rascally, self-seeking lot they were too, looked at from the height of Denestornya Castle.

Count Balint Abady, the Lord of Denestornya and of great tracts of forest and farmland besides, is the trilogy's hero. Young, debonair, but also serious-minded, he is full of goodwill. He knows all the local titled families but is also grander, having connections beyond Transylvania and having been to school in Vienna. This makes him feel an outsider. His cousin and friend, Count Laszlo Gyeroffy, shares this uncomfortable feeling, but to a greater degree.

In the early parts of the novel, before Laszlo descends into alcoholism, we accompany the cousins as they variously negotiate the pleasures, excitements or tedium of society, with its balls, races and grand shooting parties. Numerous sub-plots thread their way through these events against the backgrounds of the servants' quarters, the gaming tables, a charity bazaar, a shooting lodge, the foresters' encampment. The characters crackle with energy, much of it springing from their malicious or eccentric personalities. Hungarians, says Banffy, love the ridiculous, and there is plenty of evidence of that here. The varied landscapes become almost an additional character in the narrative. In its precise description and painterly detail, the novel often reads like good travel writing.

Two themes, however, take centre stage: love and politics. Balint's slowly blossoming but doomed affair with a married woman runs through the trilogy almost from beginning to end. He gets within an ace of what he so dearly wants – the chance to marry Adrienne and have an heir to Denestornya – only to have it snatched away on the eve of war. Banffy was right to deny him his heir. The age of aristocratic paternalism was coming to an end. Any heirs Balint might have had would not have been allowed to hold on to their inheritance for long.

Banffy's zest for politics takes up a fair bit of the book, which may be why he has been compared to Trollope. He had already been a diplomat, an MP and in 1921–2 Hungary's Foreign Minister, before despair at the venal ways of the political world led him to become a writer instead. His Balint is a patriotic Hungarian, distrustful of Vienna, in favour of universal suffrage but inclined to view demonstrating workers as rabble whipped up by demagogues – upstart lawyers, probably. In his lofty, trusting way, he does his best to help the Romanian peasants by encouraging co-operatives.

By the novel's end Balint has many reasons to be broken-hearted. Rather than take a soft option offered him in Vienna, he enlists for the war. The scene in which he leaves his ancestral home, making sure that everything is left in good order, is poignant. First he bids farewell to the animals, then he leads us through the gardens and orchards and into all the rooms of the castle with memories dear to him.

The conclusion of the novel is datelined 'Bonczhida, May 20th, 1940'. Bonczhida was the real castle upon which the fictional Denestornya was based. Presumably, when Banffy wrote that scene of leave-taking, he was at home and everything was still in place. Enacting that last tour in his mind may have been a presentiment. The castle was later burned down by the Nazis in reprisal for Banffy's suggestion that Hungary should sue for a separate peace with the Allies.

At least in one respect, fate was kinder to him than to his fictional counterpart. He had one daughter, Katalin Banffy-Jelen. It is through her work and that of her co-translator, Patrick Thursfield, that we can now read this grand novel in English. It was only a will-o'-the wisp feeling that drew me to it, based on nothing more substantial than a tone of voice, the sense of a particular time. But I'm delighted that it did, because reading the trilogy opens up and restores a whole world, just as Banffy hoped it would.

RUTH PAVEY is a journalist who writes on fiction, gardening and contemporary crafts, and a teacher, working in inner London with refugee children and their parents. Other unequal struggles include trying to play the cello and to restore a derelict orchard in Somerset.

A Perfect Nightmare

LUCY LETHBRIDGE

In 1935, Denton Welch – then an art student at Goldsmith's College
– was knocked off his bike on a busy road just outside Bromley. He
spent over a year in hospital and was permanently weakened by his
injuries. He died thirteen years later at the age of 33, leaving behind
him a few strange but compelling books – all of which obsessively
pick over Denton's recollections of his life before the accident. They
culminate in *A Voice through a Cloud*, a nightmarish account of his
months in hospitals and convalescent homes in southern England.
He died before he finished it and it ends, with poignant abruptness,
in the middle of a paragraph, with Denton sitting, uncertain and
in pain, in his doctor's car which is parked outside a bungalow in
Broadstairs.

    A Voice, and Welch's other best-known book *Maiden Voyage*, are
generally described as novels, probably because they do not seem to
fit into any other category. Yet there is no fiction in Welch: everything in his writing is refracted through the broken mirror of his own
experience, and recounted in the first person in his own peculiar,

Denton Welch, *A Voice through A Cloud* (1950)
Enitharmon Press · Hb · 230pp · £15 · ISBN 1904634060
The decorative heading is by Denton Welch and was used in the first edition.

inimitable voice. *Maiden Voyage* is an account of Denton's running away from boarding school, then going out to China where his father was the director of a lumber company in Shanghai. It was the first Denton Welch I ever read and was given to me by a boyfriend. I was gripped by its narrator's odd-angled eye on the world, but it was a weird kind of book to give as a love token: fastidious, snobbish, voyeuristic and intensely self-absorbed, Welch appears to be more concerned with objects than people.

He was the kind of child who, while his friends were playing cricket, was polishing his parents' antique furniture, rearranging his collection of ivory snuffboxes or sifting through his mother's jewellery. From an early age, a lustreware teapot could send him into raptures. His narrative voice was confidently established from the first in a quite brilliant account of going to tea with Walter Sickert in 1936 (published in *Horizon*). 'I remember with a vividness the slight shock I received on being confronted with a glistening white WC, as soon as the door was opened.' Later we find Denton slyly turning over the Sickerts' silver teaspoons to check the hallmark.

But although Welch's world often seems composed only of surfaces, the reader soon finds that his apparently artless, surreal juxtapositions reveal deep feelings of fear and longing. His memories of his own few golden years are an elegy for an England now vanished – teashops, church-crawling, antique-shop treasures, lovely, unselfconscious farm boys stripping off to plunge into rivers after a day's labour – but it is also touched by a sense of creeping uncertainty and fear: 'The castle at Chilham, perched on its hill in the heart of the trees, brought back my tiredness under the hot sun, my sense of isolation in a world of motor cars and melting tar.'

In *A Voice through a Cloud* this uncertainty comes to a head in ruthlessly dissected horrors – it is as if, sensing the imminence of his own death, Welch was saving the worst for last. The book begins on a Whitsun bank holiday as Denton sets out on his bicycle to visit his uncle in his Surrey vicarage. On the outskirts of Beckenham he stops to have tea in an eighteenth-century house which he describes with characteristic Pevsner-like attention to detail, recoiling at the way the proportions of the room have been ruined by the tea urn and the gaudy advertisements. He gets back on his bicycle and minutes later is run down by a car, waking up in a hospital unable to feel his legs.

Welch has an extraordinary gift for description. His writing is spare and precise and he has a brilliant knack for the spot-on simile that brings one up short. Sometimes he overdoes it and tips over into the lurid, but this is rare. Edith Sitwell, one of his mentors, on whom he poured lavish adoration in his journals, wrote quite rightly that Welch 'never fumbles'. The horrors in *A Voice* come thick and fast, but they are intensely vivid and made more so by the curious, separated voice in which they are recounted. In the next-door hospital bed to Welch is a man whose girlfriend visits him. She is lame and, when she brushes back her hair, he sees she has no ear, only a gaping hole. 'She appeared to me as the victim of some horrible medieval brutality.' Yet while the other patients look on her with compassion, Welch is struck by the unsentimental nature of his neighbour.

> He told me about his marriage plans, the council flat and the increased pay he hoped for. I tried to look under his words for something hidden, something more; but each plain statement refused to be given more depth or colouring. His girl was his girl. She had no ear. She had a game leg. They had no house or flat yet. He hadn't enough money yet. Still, they would be married. No more thought need be wasted on the matter.

We do not know what his fellow-patients thought of Denton Welch, but he must have been disconcerting to meet: camp, waspish, tremblingly thin-skinned – at least when it came to himself – perhaps whipping out an exercise book to note down observations of his company and their conversations. Though he was quick to pour scorn on the taste and pieties of the bourgeoisie, he held firm to a few bourgeois prejudices himself – one nurse, a novice Catholic priest, he describes as 'a great black tarantula in cassock and biretta, with hairy spider ankles'.

Yet for me anyway, despite all this, he makes one see the world through his curious personal kaleidoscope, all the pieces shaken into a new, sometimes jangling pattern of shapes and colours. In the end, one's feelings of irritation (even sometimes repugnance) are out-weighed by sympathy for Welch's loneliness and admiration for his art which, for all its over-wrought aestheticism and its self-conscious-ness, is always painfully honest.

In *A Voice*, Denton tells us of the daydream with which he fills the long days in hospital. In a world reduced to a white bed and to excruciating pain, he has created a characteristically Welchian conso-lation – a perfect room, with no one else there to spoil the effect and everything in it beautiful and placed there for its own perfect pur-pose: a winged armchair covered in old needlework, a kitten, candles in silver sconces, a delicious tea of toast and one speckled brown egg, a dish of jam made with white cherries.

One can imagine Denton lovingly developing every detail of this daydream in the sanitary chilliness and horror of the hospital. All in this dream room is perfectly in its place and aesthetically pleasing; nothing is excessive – there is just one brown egg. And there at the centre of it all sits Denton, with his antique sconces and his white cherries a shield against the vulgarities of the outside world. Reading Denton Welch has always made me feel like a Peeping Tom, looking through the window of that room with a melancholy, sometimes hor-rified fascination – all the while knowing that, despite its appearance of intimacy, I, the reader, am unlikely to be invited to enter.

LUCY LETHBRIDGE's books for children include biographies of Ada Lovelace (*The Computer Wizard of Victorian England*) and Annie Oakley (*Sharpshooter of the Wild West*). She is the literary editor of *The Tablet*.

Made in Siberia

JOHN DE FALBE

Every season a couple of wonderful biographies emerge whose reviews and sales might lead one to believe that they will stay bestsellers for ever. A year or two later they are in no greater demand than thousands of other backlist titles. Examples of this might be Amanda Foreman's *Georgiana* or David Gilmour's *Curzon*. Both were rightly acclaimed, but after the flurry of reviews, after Christmas had come and gone, they joined others on the shelves as definitive works on rather specialized subjects whose future sales will be steady, but modest. This is not to derogate the books: it is just what happens.

There is another type of book, which may not have made such a splash in the media on publication but which a bookseller is likely to keep within reach of the till for a quick response to the question, 'Can you recommend a good biography?' Such books may be personal favourites and they are liable also to be more personal in content. They probably won't depend on any extraneous knowledge for enjoyment. At one extreme might be *The Last Leopard* (David Gilmour again), a superb biography of Lampedusa that makes vivid the inner drama of a writer's life. At the other end lies perhaps Joe Simpson's *Touching the Void*, the story of a mountaineering accident in the Andes whose drama turns on a harrowing dilemma.

Somewhere along the scale lie Axel Munthe's *The Story of San Michele* and books by a tough, self-sufficient sisterhood of plucky women: *The Past Is Myself* (Christabel Bielenberg), *A Mother's War*

Christine Sutherland, *The Princess of Siberia* (1984)
Quartet · Pb · 326pp · £8 · ISBN 0704381621

(Fey von Hassell), *The House by the Dvina* (Eugenie Fraser), and *The Berlin Diaries* ('Missie' Vassiltchikov). My own clear favourite in this group is Christine Sutherland's *The Princess of Siberia*. As a well-researched historical biography, it has the authority of good history, but its brilliance lies in the personal nature of its focus, its skilful unpicking of the emotional threads binding its characters. It is an amazing story to whose broader cultural significance the author is alert, and a dream subject for a biography.

In December 1825, on the first day of Tsar Nicholas I's reign, an ill-conceived revolution by a group of idealistic young aristocrats ended in disaster. When the enquiry finished a year later, five of the ringleaders were hanged; 120 were sent to Siberia, most of them for life, with varying sentences of hard labour. The affair was without political consequence (although it might be argued that it set back the cause of reform in Russia for years because of its effect on Nicholas I). It merits no more than a few pages in Seton-Watson's mammoth *The Russian Empire, 1801–1917*, but even he allows that the Decembrists were among 'the bravest, ablest, and most attractive sons, perhaps the noblest figures in the whole history of Russian revolutionary action'.

Christine Sutherland's Princess is Maria Raevsky, the favourite daughter of General Raevsky, who features in *War and Peace* as the hero of Borodino. Rich and well-connected, as a teenager Maria also knew the young Pushkin well. When she became engaged to Prince Sergei Volkonsky, one of the Tsar's aides-de-camp, it was regarded as a superb match by everyone except her father, who was aware that Sergei's membership of a secret society might get him into trouble.

Despite the General's misgivings, Maria and Volkonsky did marry. A year later, when Maria's son was born, she had not seen her husband for two weeks. It was another three months before anyone told her that he was incarcerated in the Peter and Paul Fortress. Far from disowning her husband, as her family wished, Maria declared that she would follow him to Siberia. His arrest and the causes for which he had been arrested (constitutional reform, the abolition of serfdom) made sense of behaviour that had puzzled her: her romantic leanings suddenly gained form and clarity. It was made very difficult for Maria to join her husband: she had to leave behind her baby, renounce her wealth, title and even the prospect of returning to Russia. But

Maria, by Nikolai Bestuzhev

she was not alone: 'eleven wives of the condemned prisoners decided to share the fate of their husbands. Six of them were forced to leave behind a total of thirteen children.'

After an epic journey to Siberia, Maria settled down in a shack in Nerchinsk with the only other Decembrist wife to have arrived so far, Katyusha Trubetskoy. Accustomed to servants and wealth, the women had to learn to manage for themselves. The prisoners were not allowed any contact with the outside world, so it was the women who wrote letters to their families, mended their clothes, augmented their diet. They provided not only hope and comfort but also – because they could send information home, where they had powerful (but cautious) relations – genuine protection. After a couple of years, all the disparate groups of Decembrists were gathered together in one prison at Chita, under the rule of an improbably benign commandant called Leparsky. This enabled them to survive as a group beyond political death (although the Tsar's motive for putting them under one roof was to separate them from others).

In Chita they set about educating one another and the local community, helped by books and periodicals obtained through the women. It was not to last: the 'Chita Academy' was disbanded and the prisoners moved to a larger, permanent, specially built prison at Petrovsky Zavod. As the compassionate Leparsky grew confident that his charges understood the ground rules – 'Behave, and I will let you lead as much of a life as I can' – the prisoners were allowed to visit their wives' houses and the wives to share their husbands' cells. Children were born, gardens made, Buriat dictionaries compiled, lectures given. And as Volkonsky became eccentric and prematurely aged, Maria took as her lover another of the Decembrists, an old family friend called Poggio.

But it is the connections that make this book so fascinating. The abortive revolution struck deep into the highest layer of society. These were the fast-trackers from the Napoleonic wars, the ones who had returned from France with rosy futures, but instead of lapsing back complacently into Russian absolutism, they believed that the time had come to reform Russia. They all knew one another, and if their brothers and cousins were not Decembrists too then they were high officials. So one of the ringleaders at Nerchinsk with Volkonsky was Maria's uncle, Vasya Davydov. Volkonsky's mother was Mistress of the Robes to the Dowager Empress, and was dancing with the Tsar at a party given by Prince Kochubey as her son left St Petersburg in chains for Siberia. A generation later, Maria's daughter Elena married a Prince Kochubey. General Benckendorff, the chief of police who was instrumental in sending the conspirators to Siberia, was an old school companion of Sergei's.

After Volkonsky's term of hard labour had come to an end he was sent to live in Urik, a village near Irkutsk. A few years later Maria was allowed to move into Irkutsk with their two children. Thanks to Muraviev, the new governor of Eastern Siberia (who had eight cousins among the Decembrists), Maria was given access to some of her family's money, so that she lived in Irkutsk in some style. She helped finance the local foundling home and hospital and built a concert hall; much loved, she became known as the Princess of Siberia. There is a wonderful moment when Sergei's sister comes to visit after twenty-five years. She is a *grande dame* of the old school, but after a concert it is Maria, the wife of a state criminal, who is given a standing ovation.

Eventually Tsar Nicholas died and his son, Alexander II, announced an amnesty for the Decembrists. Maria never properly settled back into life in the West – Siberia was the making of her – and she died seven years later, in 1863. Surprisingly, Sergei flourished on his return: having become notorious among the Decembrists for being uncouth and unkempt, interested only in farming and peasants, he brushed up nicely and was regarded as a grand old man; he died in 1865. Poggio, an attractive character who may have fathered Maria's daughter, died in 1873 and was buried beside Sergei and Maria.

Although many Decembrists died miserably in remote places, some of them returned to Russia in old age as legendary figures. Tolstoy (whose grandfather was a Volkonsky) met Sergei and was certainly influenced by him. It is impossible not to see Pierre Bezukhov as a prototype Decembrist. But if the Decembrists did not quite suffer the living death that Nicholas intended, that had less to do with Tolstoy than with Alexander Herzen, who kept alive their collective identity from his own exile. The triumph of Tom Stoppard's extraordinary trilogy, *The Coast of Utopia*, was to show how Herzen's private life was entangled with his intellectual life, and how he struggled to remain true to both. It is no wonder that he revered the Decembrists, whose personal lives, as Christine Sutherland so eloquently reveals, were integral to the drama of their story and to their ultimate legacy.

JOHN DE FALBE has sold books at John Sandoe's in Chelsea for nearly twenty years. He is the author of two novels, *The Glass Night* and *The Bequest*, the latter of which came out in paperback in November. He also reviews books regularly for *The Spectator*.

High Life

SEBASTIAN HORSLEY

Bad News by Edward St Aubyn is, quite simply, the best book ever written about drugs. Thomas de Quincey, Charles Baudelaire, Jean Cocteau, William Burroughs, Hunter S. Thompson, Irvine Welsh and Will Self may all be writers roped together like mountaineers heading for the summit, but it is St Aubyn they will find at the top. I first came across the book about five years ago. There it was, quietly glowing away on a friend's shelf. And from the moment I picked it up I knew it was a work of perfection. It fitted my own experience as seamlessly as a silk glove.

Bad News is the second book in St Aubyn's Patrick Melrose trilogy. Each part covers one day in the life of its protagonist – days that encapsulate the causes, the consequences and the resolution of a cruelly damaged childhood. Patrick Melrose is physically abused by his father, becomes a junkie and then tries to seek redemption after going straight.

The first book, *Never Mind*, set in the South of France, examines a family who find themselves trapped like spiders in a bottle, forced to devour one another. *Bad News* takes Patrick to New York to pick up his deceased father's ashes, and traces his descent into narcotic oblivion. The last, *Some Hope*, is an excoriating attack on upper-class English society, seen as it descends upon a marquee in the country for a grand dinner party at which Princess Margaret is present.

Edward St Aubyn, *Never Mind* (1992); *Bad News* (1992); *Some Hope* (1994)
Published together as *The Patrick Melrose Trilogy* (1998)
Minerva · Pb · 560pp · £9.99 · ISBN 0099274507

Patrick, who has now given up drugs, makes a merciless spectator.

Each part is brilliant. But it is the second that unlocked images for me, for I looked into its dark mirror and saw myself.

By the time I was in my thirties crack had taken me like an eagle grabbing a rabbit. Heroin was the elixir that soothed my senses and brought me back down to earth. I took drugs as an escape from a life I found unendurable. I took drugs because I enjoyed taking them. The fixing ritual becomes the sweetest form of pleasure – the needle, the belt round the arm, the powder in the spoon, the flame applied. The chemical sweeps around your body like a torch-lit procession. You hear the angels sing. And often, by my side as I lay in this abyss of sensuality, was St Aubyn's book. Even stoned I knew you must always read stuff that would make you look good if you were to die in the middle of it.

Reading *Bad News* when I was clean, one of the things that astonished me was St Aubyn's ability to capture the actual effects of drugs, and not simply describe the lifestyle as other writers have done. 'Heroin landed purring at the base of his skull, and wrapped itself darkly around his nervous system, like a black cat curling up on its favourite cushion. It was as soft and rich as the throat of a wood-pigeon or the splash of sealing wax onto a page or a handful of gems slipping from palm to palm,' he writes. He describes cocaine as 'the arctic landscape of pure terror', a feeling of being 'empty and fragile as a pane of glass'.

St Aubyn dissects society with cruel, exquisite precision. But he is savagely, satirically, wickedly funny too. Take the passage when Patrick, having travelled to New York to pick up his father's ashes, finds himself storming down Madison Avenue with his father, in a brown paper bag, on his arm.

> By the time he reached Sixty-First Street, Patrick realized that it was the first time he had been alone with his father for more than ten minutes without being buggered, hit, or insulted . . .

The tragedy of old age, when a man is too weak to hit his own child. No wonder he had died. Even his rudeness had been flagging towards the end, and he had been forced to introduce a note of repulsive self-pity to ward off any counter-attack.

One of the reasons Kafka's 'The Metamorphosis' works so brilliantly is because Gregor never questions why he has awoken one morning 'transformed into a gigantic insect'. By the same token Patrick never questions why he has become a drug addict. He just has. He is attractive because he appears genuinely to despair of life while never, ever whining about it. Self-pity is, of course, the most destructive of the non-pharmaceutical narcotics. The trouble is it is very addictive and very pleasurable. Patrick will have none of it. Indeed, it is this refusal that helps to give the books their strength.

So why is St Aubyn's work so little known here as to be almost confidential? When the trilogy was first published in America by a press so small that the secretaries probably typeset each book, it was immediately picked up by the *New York Review of Books* and given a double-page spread.

Maybe his own priorities are part of the problem. He is first and foremost a craftsman. Each sentence is honed and polished – full of bite, surprise and attack. I suspect he believes that if you produce such high-quality work, the world will beat a path to your door. It should. But it won't. Writing has become not so much a career as a personality racket. 'You have to sell yourself, just to get rid of the damned thing,' an American girlfriend tells Patrick. But Patrick – an autobiographical figure – comes from a social world in which such effort is 'vulgar'. Perhaps St Aubyn's charming inability to sell himself has the same roots. Yet as a writer he is fearless. While other authors stay on the shore, he swims out to sea. His prose is pure heroin.

SEBASTIAN HORSLEY is an artist, writer and failed suicide. He is currently working on an unauthorized autobiography called *Mein Camp*.

A Word in Your Ear

JONATHAN JAMES-MOORE

I am, literally, a bad reader. I have mild dyslexia and well remember, when reading *Peyton Place* in my youth, taking 'sonofabitch' as 'sofa-bitch' and thinking it was a piece of bordello furniture. I am also partially sighted and have difficulty reading in either bright or low light; and with poor peripheral vision I tend to miss the ends of lines. So the advent of audio tapes and of the Talking Book (pioneered by the RNIB) has been a splendid thing for me.

A conventional book provides particular pleasures – the look of the binding, the aesthetics of the typeface, the feel of the page – but a Talking Book does have one physical advantage: it is usually smaller and lighter, and so easier to pack. It leaves the listener freer, too, to respond to the ambience. Listening to a Talking Book where the only illumination is glimmering candlelight or a flickering fire is something all its own. Shadows emphasize mystery and Gothick horror, subdued light engenders romance, and comparative silence encourages confidentiality or even a sense of conspiracy with the author. I particularly recall being snowed in at New Year in an isolated country cottage where we had to resort to burning broken furniture in the stove for warmth. In these circumstances, we felt ourselves truly beleaguered in a Russian winter as we listened to Juliet Stevenson's evocative reading of *Anna Karenina*.

The quality, character and intonation of the reader's voice inevi-tably affect the listener's experience. But there is still room for the imagination to bubble and create a personal vision. As Joyce Grenfell memorably put it in her wireless criticism for the *Observer*, 'The pictures on radio are better.' I find it extraordinary that there is no

The Sofabitch, by David Eccles

acknowledged system for the notation of the spoken voice – as there is for the singing voice and even for ballet choreography. During the past two years I have been working with Stephen Greif (an actor and reader in his own right) to try to fill this gap, along with a board of assessors consisting of expert voice coaches, writers, producers and lecturers in dramatic literature.

We have now developed a system called VoiceQuality, which is being used by the Spotlight Casting Directory – their website also contains clips of actors' voices. VoiceQuality provides a lexicon of twenty adjectives to describe the quality (breathy, gentle, melodious, silky) and twenty to describe the character (amused, assured, engaging, sympathetic) of an individual's natural speaking voice. The actors choose the adjectives which they believe most nearly match their own voices, and so provide an aid to casting for audio work.

Some voices can provide good company. I'm thinking particularly of Jill Balcon's reading of *The Unequalled Self*, Claire Tomalin's wonderful biography of Samuel Pepys. Her duchess-like taffeta tones vividly conjure up both the personalities and the period. But the Royals of recorded reading are surely Miriam Margolyes and Martin Jarvis. Miriam wrests every ounce of comedy from Sue Townsend's *The Queen and I*, in which the royal family wake up to find themselves in a Republic and relocated from the Palace to a Midlands council estate. Martin Jarvis's readings of Richmal Compton's *Just William* stories are unequalled. He lightly catches the nuances of the repressed English accent and the earnestness of the aspirant middle classes, transporting us to another place and time.

Each summer I escape to my Umbrian hideaway to fulfil my listening duties as one of the judges for the unabridged fiction category of 'The Talkies', the Audio Book Publishing Association's annual awards. During the ten days I spend there listening to the shortlist, the hours reel or spin by (many books are now available on CD as well as cassette). The criteria we apply are: the suitability of the title for audio; the quality of the reader's performance; and overall enjoyment and ease of use. The range of the shortlist is remarkable, although thrillers and mystery seem to predominate. There is a lot of blood on the cassette deck.

In 2003, however, the two that worked best for me were *A Month in the Country* by J.L. Carr, read by Nick Rawlinson, and *Embers* by Sándor Márai, read by Paul Scofield and sensitively produced by John Tydeman. *A Month in the Country* centres on the restoration of a medieval wall painting in a Yorkshire church by a traumatized First World War survivor. In *Embers*, set in the last days of the Austro-Hungarian Empire, a dying aristocrat entertains his late wife's lover to dinner in his echoing schloss. Paul Scofield's golden voice gives perfect weight and meaning to each syllable, powerfully evoking a whole life and the passing of an Empire. Both these novels are par-ticularly suited to the Talking Book format since they are first-person narratives, making a direct connection between reader and listener.

In 2004, a semi-dramatized comedy science fiction, *The AntiPope*, jostled on the shortlist with two Agatha Christies (*Endless Night* and *The Pale Horse*), a Daphne du Maurier (*I'll Never Be Young Again*), Joe David Brown's *Paper Moon*, a rites-of-passage story set in the American Depression of the 1930s, and Sarah Cauldwell's intriguing thriller *The Sirens Sang of Murder*, the comedy of which was highlighted by Eva Haddon's witty and wry delivery. This novel moves between Lincoln's Inn Fields and the Channel Islands as we are invited to unravel the motives for murder in the convoluted world of tax avoidance trusts. It certainly provided the requisite pools of blood, as did *Country of the Blind*, Christopher Brookmire's take on the unsavoury world of the media barons.

However, it was the Irish last year who took the category to a sublime level. First, there was Dermot Crowley and Sean Barrett's masterly reading of Samuel Beckett's *Molloy*. Crowley delivers Beckett's archetypal tramp as if he has actually lived the life, while Barrett brings a satirical edge to the journal of the tramp's provincial tracker. The narrative is secondary to the words themselves, heard as sound, free of meaning, yet full of humour and satire.

However in the end, for me, it was Jim Norton and Marcella Riordan's stunning rendering of James Joyce's complete and un-abridged *Ulysses* that won the day. Norton effortlessly inhabits a huge range of characters, while Marcella Riordan is a roisterous, raunchy Molly Bloom. This mind-bending, ear-stretching twenty-seven and a half hours is longer even than Bloomsday itself. Appropriately, I listened to it on the centenary – 16 June 2004. It is a *tour de force*, making a great but difficult work accessible. I was genuinely sorry when it was over, bereft at the loss of so many amusing and frank friends.

Audio books have moved on from being a service for the blind or deputizing for a parent reading a bedtime story, or even a way of trying to silence children on long car journeys. They are available in many bookshops, but the specialist is the now well-established Talking Bookshop in London's Wigmore Street.

JONATHAN JAMES-MOORE read Engineering at Cambridge, or rather just looked at the diagrams. Lured by the stage, he spent ten years as a theatre manager, joining the BBC in 1978 where, by a process of erosion – all other talent having left for TV – he rose to be Head of Light Entertainment, Radio. He now works as a freelance audio producer.

The Talking Bookshop, 11 Wigmore Street, London W1U 1PE, tel 020 7491 4117, fax 020 7629 1966, freephone 0800 074 5086, e-mail support@talkingbooks. co.uk, www.talkingbooks.co.uk

Posh but Down-to-Earth

URSULA BUCHAN

Recently, I noticed a rather irritating poster on the Underground proclaiming: 'You never forget your first time.' It was an advertisement for a villa holiday company – bizarrely – but the irritation I felt (since I am not annoyed by villa holidays per se) had to do with the too obvious double entendre. In fact, one does not forget the first time that one does quite a lot of things – seeing one's name in print, for instance, or walking along Striding Edge, that most vertiginous of paths on to the top of Helvellyn – and certainly I have never forgotten the first time I read a gardening book.

I was only 20, and still at university, when I was given *V. Sackville-West's Garden Book* by a friend, a first-rate gardener who was keen to encourage my burgeoning interest. I see from the flyleaf that she hoped I would be 'as delighted and inspired by this book' as she was. Yes, indeed. I had never read anything like it. Gardening advice then meant Percy Thrower and Arthur Billitt – extraordinary characters who looked in the 1970s as if they had landed in a time capsule from the Edwardian era – together with *Roses: Their Culture and Management*, a book which lived for many years in the downstairs loo, where it was definitely read more as a way of passing the time than for pleasure. To come across a writer, therefore, on such an unpromising subject, who spoke immediately and directly to the reader in an easy yet cultured style, was a revelation.

V. Sackville-West, *In Your Garden* (1951) and *In Your Garden Again* (1953)
Frances Lincoln · Hb · 240pp and 176pp · £14.99 each ·
ISBNS 0711223548 and 0711223556

V. Sackville-West's Garden Book, published by Michael Joseph, was an anthology compiled from four earlier books – *In Your Garden* (1951), *In Your Garden Again* (1953), *More for Your Garden* (1955) and *Even More for Your Garden* (1958). These were themselves anthologies of the best of her immensely popular weekly *Observer* articles, which had appeared since 1947 and were to continue until 1961, the year before she died. (When I began to write for the *Observer* in 1986, I found that there were still readers around who had principally taken the newspaper in order to read her gardening columns, and who rather

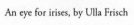

An eye for irises, by Ulla Frisch

wished she was still doing them. There was also a sub-editor working there who was rather glad she was not, since she had apparently hated changes being made to her copy.)

These articles nearly all referred to her garden at Sissinghurst in Kent, which she and her husband, the diplomat-turned-writer Sir Harold Nicolson, had laid out from 1930. They covered her successes and failures, the plants she liked, the ideas she had; in short, the small bright coinage of gardening life, new-minted by a very good practical gardener and plantsman. Her articles gave the impression that she was a woman leading a quiet, orderly country life, spending her time filling in seed orders and going out to deadhead roses in the evening, when in fact her private life could still sometimes be tumultuous, if not on the scale it had been before the war.

The book I was given in 1973 is long since out of print, but last spring Frances Lincoln reissued the two earliest, and best, collections, *In Your Garden* and *In Your Garden Again*. Both are essentially anthologies of the *Observer* articles, except that the first contains other writings as well, including an excellent extended essay on

Hidcote Manor, reprinted from a 1949 issue of the *RHS Journal*. The books are facsimiles of the originals, which gives them a distinct and pleasantly period feel. I had not read either of these collections since the mid-1980s, so I picked them up with just that same sense of anticipation I get when picking up an Anne Tyler, say. I know what to expect and know it won't disappoint.

Take the entry for 18 June 1950, for example, when she first writes about her famous thyme lawn:

> Two years ago, I had what I thought might be a bright idea. It has turned out so bright, in both senses of the word, that I must pass it on.
>
> I had two small windswept beds . . . divided by a path of paving stones down the middle. I tried every sort of thing in them, including a mad venture of hollyhocks, which, of course, got flattened by the prevailing south-west wind, however strongly we staked them. So then I decided I must have something very low growing, which would not suffer from the wind, and scrapped the hollyhocks, and dibbled in lots and lots of thyme, and now have a sort of lawn which, while it is densely flowering in purple and red, looks like a Persian carpet laid flat on the ground out of doors. The bees think that I have laid it for their especial benefit. It really is a lovely sight; I do not want to boast, but I cannot help being pleased with it; it is so seldom that one's experiments in gardening are wholly successful.

Or how about this on the Algerian iris, *Iris unguicularis*?

> You should search your clumps of the grass-like leaves every day for possible buds, and pull the promising bud while it still looks like a tiny, tightly-rolled umbrella, and then bring it indoors and watch it open under a lamp. If you have the patience to wait long enough, you will see this miracle happen.

Of course, these essays can be uneven – sometimes a little patronizing to her readers, and occasionally obviously dashed off. You can see that the Sunday morning task could sometimes be a chore, rather than a pleasure. But I think you can tell she often enjoyed connecting with fellow-gardeners, many of whom had no inkling that she was an aristocrat, living in the middle of an enormous, complex garden, who wrote her weekly articles halfway up a stately Tudor tower.

She was a self-taught amateur, like them, but one who could lift her readers' eyes towards horizons they might otherwise not have seen. She wrote in a light, accessible, excited and, at times, attractively diffident manner. She was sympathetic, honest and positive. She rarely dwelt on plants she did not like, except the rose 'American Pillar', which she could not stand. Who can? Best of all, although the canvas on which she worked was large, she painted pictures with small groups of plants, so that her ideas could be translated to much smaller gardens than her own.

When I was 20, and had never read anything on gardening before, I was enchanted by Vita's light-hearted seriousness and practical romanticism, and have uncritically championed her ever since, despite a gradual realization that she was not that original. She was influenced in particular by Gertrude Jekyll (the White Garden and all), and William Robinson, and I suspect Norah Lindsay and Lawrence Johnston as well. The structure of the garden at Sissinghurst – as she would freely admit – was Harold Nicolson's triumph, not hers. That said, no gardening writer, before or since, has had more power to delight or inspire. And I rather doubt I would be a gardening journalist now, if I had not read Vita first of all.

URSULA BUCHAN writes on gardening for *The Spectator* and the *Daily Telegraph*. Like Vita Sackville-West, her gardening journalism has been collected into anthologies – *Good in a Bed* and *Better Against a Wall* – but there she fears the similarity ends.

Peacock's Progress

J.W.M THOMPSON

The ups and downs of literary reputations are often slightly mysterious. I still find it strange, though, that although we pay ample homage to most of the heavyweights of the nineteenth century, one of the best and liveliest of them all has been allowed to fade from view. Thomas Love Peacock (1785–1866) deserves much better than that. I find his writings – sceptical, dry and sparkling with wit – as rewarding today as when I first read them many years ago.

Perhaps a present-day reader coming fresh to his novels should be warned that they resemble those of no other writer. Peacock pretty well invented a form new to English literature, the 'Peacockian novel', a kind of hybrid between conversation and narrative. He also invented a private world: an attractive and comfortable world it is too, where a continuous intellectual comedy takes place in a setting of Arcadian landscape.

Peacock's method is to assemble a gaggle of opinionated characters at a country house, supply them with a more or less preposterous plot, and then let them indulge in a feast of disputatious talk. They eat and drink merrily, take walks to admire the scenery, make expeditions by boat – but the talk is the main thing. Each participant has his own crotchet ('a whimsical fancy, a perverse conceit' – *OED*) and propounds it with vigour. In this genial way Peacock satirizes the crazes and trendy notions of his time (not essentially unlike those of

Thomas Love Peacock, *Headlong Hall* (1816) · Pb · £11.95 · ISBN 1592243452; *Crotchet Castle* (1831) · Pb · £13.95 · ISBN 1587156679 Both available print-on-demand from Wildside Press, USA today). He has influenced some later writers. Aldous Huxley called *Crome Yellow* his Peacockian novel, choosing the thinly disguised Garsington Manor of Lady Ottoline Morrell for its setting.

Peacock was sometimes called the court jester of the Romantic movement, and some of his characters bear a mocking resemblance 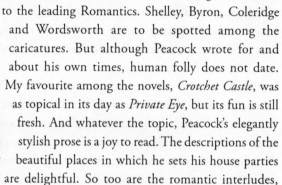 to the leading Romantics. Shelley, Byron, Coleridge and Wordsworth are to be spotted among the caricatures. But although Peacock wrote for and about his own times, human folly does not date. My favourite among the novels, *Crotchet Castle*, was as topical in its day as *Private Eye*, but its fun is still fresh. And whatever the topic, Peacock's elegantly stylish prose is a joy to read. The descriptions of the beautiful places in which he sets his house parties are delightful. So too are the romantic interludes, which he presents in a half-serious, half-amused way. One feels that he wrote, as he should be read, for pleasure.

Idiosyncratic: Peacock, by Mark Handley

A typically engaging character is Dr Folliott, who dominates the dinner table at Crotchet Castle much in the manner of Dr Johnson, specializing in delivering amiable blasts of good sense. Often, of course, he is a mouthpiece for Peacock's own robust opinions. One fellow-diner, baffled by a speech from this character in which Coleridge is lampooned, says sadly, 'I have read the divine Kant, sir, with an anxious desire to understand him; and I confess I have not succeeded.' Dr Folliott explains the problem neatly: 'He wants the two great requisites of head and tail.'

Peacock is happy when satirizing the 'march of mind', in his day the fashionable term for Progress, which, as Dr Folliott knew and we know, is all too often in the wrong direction. His barbs land on busybody politicians and bureaucrats who prosper at the public expense, as well as on transcendental philosophers whose obscurities numb the mind. One might wonder how, while making comedy out of the poets and thinkers of his acquaintance, he remained on good terms with them. I imagine this was because he was never unkind to his victims personally. Instead he made fun of their wild ideas and intellectual extravagances. His friendship with Shelley (an entirely different sort of person) was surprisingly close and he was named as the poet's executor; yet he once wrote, of his days with the Shelleys and their circle, that he was 'irreverent enough to laugh at the fervour with which opinions utterly unconducive to any practical result were battled for as matters of the highest importance'. Such was the essential Peacockian attitude.

His idiosyncratic style was revealed plainly in the very first of his novels, *Headlong Hall*. This has the usual assortment of crotcheteers in a country house, in this case among the mountains of Wales. We meet Mr Escot, the 'deteriorationist', whose denunciation of false Progress is positively Swiftian: 'These improvements, as you call them, appear to be only so many links in the great chain of corruption, which will soon fetter the whole human race in slavery.'

So much for the Industrial Revolution. Mr Escot reminds me of Dr Opimian, a character in the last of the Peacock novels, *Gryll Grange*, who declares: 'Science is an edged tool with which men play like children and cut their own fingers . . . I almost think it is the ultimate destiny of science to exterminate the human race.' That was thought atrociously reactionary in 1860. We can less comfortably dismiss it today. Against Mr Escot are set Mr Foster, the 'perfectibilarian', who rejoices in 'the progress of the species towards moral and intellectual perfection', and a third guest of Squire Headlong, Mr Jenkinson, the 'status-quo-ite'. All three argue (in elegant Peacockian language) for and against progress, and much else.

Peacock was himself as ripe a character as any he depicted. He left school at an early age, attended no university, but by solitary study turned himself into a notable classical scholar and man of letters. He had a poor opinion of the universities of his day (one of his characters refers caustically to 'the undisturbed libraries' of Oxford) and, thanks to modest private means, his early adult years were passed in agreeable idleness, studying, travelling and writing poetry. Eventually the money dried up, so Peacock found employment with the East India Company, where his brains and an unexpected gift for administration took him right to the top. He ended up as the equivalent of a modern Whitehall mandarin, secure and well-rewarded.

Clearly he had a fondness for accomplished young women. They usually shine in his novels as beacons of sense amid the fog of disputation. *Crotchet Castle* contains the delightful Clarinda, whose droll and witty teasing of a besotted suitor is clever and funny. When Peacock himself felt able to take a wife he proposed by letter to a girl he had met in Wales eight years earlier and had not seen since: a nicely Peacockian romance. The marriage was happy, although his bride's health was not good.

It was an unpredictable life story, in which the footloose poet was transmogrified into a pillar of society. Happily the satirist within him flourished undimmed, and his talent for witty appraisal of the follies of the world never weakened. It is a shame that the modern world of publishing should show so little interest in him and his works.

J.W.M.THOMPSON now lives in rural Norfolk, but he thinks his years in Fleet Street (ten of them as Editor of the *Sunday Telegraph*) helped him to appreciate Peacock's interest in the dottier aspects of human nature.

A Past Relived

SUE BRIDGWATER

I first read Alison Uttley's *The Country Child* over thirty years ago, when I was already in my twenties. I have always remembered it fondly, for it described a way of life that did not then seem so very far away. My grandmother was born in 1897 and I could still remember her stories of life on a remote Devon farm. When the book was re-issued recently I read it again, this time with the eyes of a children's librarian, wondering whether it would appeal to those brought up in very different times and from very different backgrounds.

Alison Uttley – author, too, of the much-loved *Little Grey Rabbit* and *Sam Pig* books – was born in 1884, at Castle Top Farm near Cromford in Derbyshire, and her novel evokes, in magical detail, a childhood in late Victorian rural England. It is a world where farm work is done by men and horses and seasonal Irish labourers, where the servants sit below the salt and the farmhand at the dresser; where the local squire may take over your land and house for a day while he and his guests go hunting. Here, water comes from clean-flowing streams, and larders are full of home-brewed, home-preserved, home-baked and home-bottled food.

The story, which follows a year in the life of the farm, is told from the viewpoint of Susan Garland, an only child living at remote Windystone Hall, for which Alison Uttley's own Castle Top Farm was the model. Having no other children to play with, Susan relies on the daily routines of the farm, the adults around her, the minute details

Alison Uttley, *The Country Child* (1931) · Illustrated by C. F. Tunnicliffe
Jane Nissen Books · Pb · 216pp · £6.99 · ISBN 1903252016

of animal and plant-life in the fields and
woods and hedges, for her amusement
and education. The house and farm seem
charged with life, and with the presence
of those who have gone before, stretch-
ing right back to the Saxons and the
Romans.

But though the book is set in another
age, the feelings it describes are timeless. How superficially unlike a modern
child's visit to the circus is the outing
Susan's family takes, all dressed in their
very best in a pony trap hung with lan-
terns. The lions and elephants are like
creatures from another planet to this
audience, while to the modern child they
are familiar almost to the point of ennui
from endless television documentaries. Yet how well I recognized
Susan's reaction to the clowns, for it was exactly my own in 1955.

> When the clowns came in with painted faces and baggy white
> trousers, she was much too surprised to laugh. She thought
> they were rude to the ring-master, and feared they would be
> sent away for impertinence. Her father laughed loudly at their
> sallies but she only stared, astonished.

On Christmas Day, Susan wakes in the early dark and opens her
stocking. She is just as excited as any modern child – but her presents might now seem strange: a book, an apple, a tape-measure, an
orange, nuts and a china doll. Hearing of the newfangled Christmas
tree that someone in the village has, Susan's father brings one in
and hangs it with apples, oranges, biscuits and sweets. There is the
usual turkey for dinner and cake for tea, but this Christmas day is

dominated by flickering candlelight, lantern light and firelight rather than by television, computers and flashing synchronized tree-lights. It all feels different, yet familiar too, and that is part of the fun.

Susan's mother teaches her at home until she is 7, and when she does eventually go to school, she finds it hard to fit in. She is at once odd, old-fashioned and clever.

Susan looked forward to being someone of importance . . . but her hopes were soon dashed to the ground. Mrs Garland had found in an oak chest a dress which had belonged to a girl of a bygone age . . . a brown checked woollen frock with ruches of cut material trimming the tight bodice, and edging the high neck and the flounced skirt . . . So, a quaint little old-fashioned figure . . . she went for her first day at school.

She is of course mocked for her appearance (as if, today, she were wearing the wrong 'labels') and subjected to endless questions and comments. She is jeered at and her hair is pulled. Yet eventually one or two girls are kind to her, and she learns to adjust.

Alison Uttley was herself an oddly educated child, old-fashioned even in her own time, brought up on the Bible and a few approved story-books, listening to the talk of adults who were born in the early to mid-nineteenth century, and it shows in her prose:

Then she walked down the tunnel of beech trees, for the oaks were left behind and the character of the wood had changed. The trees thinned and the beeches rose clear of undergrowth with massive smooth grey trunks from the carpet of golden leaves. Susan breathed naturally again, and walked rapidly forward, heeding neither rock nor tree, her eager eyes fixed on the light ahead. The evening sunshine streamed through the end of the path, a circle of radiance, where a stile and broken gate ended the wood.

The book is filled with similar passages where very little is happening – Susan is simply breathing and walking. So can it possibly appeal to contemporary children, who are represented in the media as creatures with poor reading skills, short attention spans and a desperate need for 'relevance', 'action' and 'accessibility'. Has *The Country Child* passed through a transition unforeseeable to its author and become an adult's book?

I don't think so. For children who like history, this is history relived. For those who like fantasy, *The Country Child* (like another of Alison Uttley's books, *A Traveller in Time*) magically reveals the closeness of the past within ancient buildings where a traditional way of life has gone on unchanged for centuries. For those who love the feeling of being transported to somewhere different when they read, this book will carry them over many years as well as miles. And for those who like detail – the long list of picnic food in *The Wind in the Willows*, Arthur Ransome's minute descriptions of stores and ropes and sails – it will be a delight. A further joy of this reprint is its reproduction of Tunnicliffe's original illustrations in which he renders the delicacy of a single flowering plant and the breadth of the landscape with equal skill.

Timeless rather than old-fashioned is how I'd describe this quiet yet eventful book. So give it to a child – but be sure to ask if you can borrow it back when he or she has finished. Better still, read it aloud to a child – especially if you are a grandparent who can say 'My grandparents told me about that.'

SUE BRIDGWATER was born in Plymouth in 1948. She is co-author of *Perian's Journey* and has also published articles and reviews on children's books and general fiction. She now lives in London.

The Book Hound

Slightly Foxed's Book Hound has run to earth a selection of interesting new fiction which may well get lost behind the piles of bestsellers.

JOHN GRIESEMER • *Signal & Noise*
This novel was published without any fanfare early last year and seems set to have an equally anonymous launch in paperback in 2005. I suspect the publisher does not know what to do with a Dickensian novel from an American actor who chooses as his subject matter the laying of the first transatlantic telegraph cable in the 1860s. Nonetheless, *Signal & Noise* is a rich and vibrant tale of industry, invention, adultery and Victorian PR which manages to move from the ocean bed to the sewers of London with wit and style, and which has already won a cult following among its small readership.

Arrow • Pb • 640pp • £7.99 • ISBN 0099460181

TAICHI YAMADA • *Strangers*
Hamada, newly divorced, runs into his parents in a Tokyo suburb and finds his life turned upside down. For Hamada was orphaned when he was 12, and the couple he now begins to visit each weekend have not aged a day since the motorbike accident that killed them thirty years before. The more time he spends with his parents the more he loses touch with the 'real' world, with the notable exception of his new girlfriend (who appears to be battling her own ghosts anyway). This is Yamada's first novel to be translated into English

and is an unusually literary ghost story which keeps you hooked right up to the truly thrilling ending.

Faber • Pb • 204pp • £9.99 • ISBN 0571224369

NIGEL HINTON • *Time Bomb*

Four friends gather together on the last day of primary school; their final day as a gang before age, and religion, take them off to new schools and new friends. One of them, Eddie, manages to get into serious trouble with the head teacher on this of all days and the four are forced to unite one more time. And then they find an unexploded bomb. It is London, 1949, and their lives are never going to be the same again. Hinton has crafted a wonderful children's novel which bears comparison with other Second World War classics such as *The Silver Sword* and *The Machine Gunners*. He manages to create believeable adult characters and to conjure up the suspicious innocence of 10-year-old boys without ever patronizing the reader.

Puffin • Pb • 276pp • £4.99 • ISBN 0141318333

ETGAR KERET • *The Nimrod Flip Out*

If your bookshelves, like mine, are somewhat lacking in the Contemporary Israeli Fiction department then look no further than this book. Keret is clearly insane and has produced one of the most bizarre collections of stories in living memory. My favourites are the one about a young man whose new girlfriend turns into a fat, beer-swilling, hairy old man every night at midnight, and the bemused narrator who has life-altering conversations with a pessimistic fish. Short-story collections have rarely been successful in this country so this book doesn't stand a hope in hell, but it deserves an audience.

Chatto & Windus • Pb • 220pp • £9.99 • ISBN 0701178094

The Tortoise and the Writer

SUE GEE

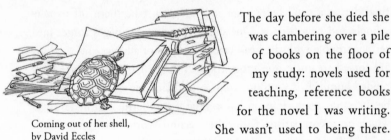

Coming out of her shell,
by David Eccles

The day before she died she was clambering over a pile of books on the floor of my study: novels used for teaching, reference books for the novel I was writing. She wasn't used to being there. She clambered over the twentieth-century fiction, and a guide to Victorian china, in the same way she did everything: slowly, with a thoughtful curiosity, and a gaze as ancient as Greece.

Her name was Archimedes. Right face, wrong gender: she looked, said my son, like an Archimedes. He named her much larger mate Homer. Homer was out in the garden, fighting fit, but Archimedes had been very ill; she was convalescing, put in a box of hay in here while I wrote, and kept an eye. Now she'd had enough of the box: she was getting out of it, getting better; I could hear the dry scrape of her feet over a little hill of paperbacks. It felt most companionable.

It had been a long cold spring. When the tortoises came out of hibernation in the cellar, they observed our London garden as they had observed it every April for the past three years, with an intelligent, clear recognition. And they set off steadily over the grass, stopping when they got tired, to go back into their shells beneath the flowering currant or forsythia. At night they slept in separate broken flowerpots.

Homer was a purposeful, active beast, always in search of food or sex; on hot summer afternoons I would hear the clack of their shells as I wrote, and look out to see them: a clumsy, extraordinary act, culminating in his clearly audible gasp. Not hers. Archimedes liked solitude. When she raised her head in the early morning air and took in the smell of wet earth, grass and compost, while the birds sang and the pear blossom spun slowly to the ground – then she was truly meditative, an ancient quiet presence that represented everything a writer needs: silence, seclusion, simplicity; time to dream.

Writers of fiction are strange creatures. We must be alert to, open to everything: each subtle shift of the human mind and heart, each complex interaction, each potential drama. This means, you might think, that we are sensitive. But writers can also have a cruel detachment and our self-absorption can be boundless. Dedication can mean exclusion: of other people, other lives.

That spring I was working on a novel in which animals featured large: dogs taken into a rural sanctuary; the sheep and cattle slaughtered during the foot-and-mouth crisis. I was writing, I was teaching, I was, in true twenty-first-century fashion, rushing about. Out in the bitter April garden, Archimedes was freezing to death.

I found her, one grey Sunday morning, on her side, tipped up as if in one last desperate struggle for warmth. If a tortoise could look ashen, she did. I knew she was on the point of death. The vet looked grave. We were given a sachet of mineral salts and a dropper, and instructions: she had to drink. She had to be kept warm indoors for at least a week. He didn't know if she would make it.

My son made her drink, prising her clamped mouth open, getting down water, drop by drop. On the second session, she opened her eyes. On the third, she opened her mouth as the dropper touched it. She was recovering; she looked about her. Caring for her became part of the day's routine. We coaxed her, we talked about her, gave bulletins to my husband at work. And we grew closer, too. It's not only animals who can be neglected when you are writing a novel.

The weather grew warmer. Archimedes was alive and active,

clambering over my books. She had been in the study for almost a week, and the garden was sunny and inviting. What could be more healing than warm fresh air? So we put her outside, for perhaps half an hour. When we brought her indoors she looked weaker, but that evening she was active again – so much so that I feared for her safety in that little box of hay. If she climbed out while we were all asleep, might she not fall, and turn fatally on her back? I put her in the cat basket, whose bars at the front offered air and safety.

Next morning I found her, at the time when she used to wake and walk out on to the dewy grass and meditate. Now her neck was stretched out between the bars, her head hung down.

We buried her beneath the buddleia, and the garden was a dreadful place. Homer walked round it over and over again. He took himself off to his flowerpot early, and his loneliness was like a shroud.

Aesop made the tortoise an iconic figure: patient, steady, filled with powers of endurance and perseverance: all the qualities required to bring a novel to completion. But it wasn't Aesop's fable I kept thinking of, in the aftermath, but D. H. Lawrence's poem 'Snake'. In the Mediterranean heat, a snake comes to the writer's water trough to drink. The writer watches, and then, on an impulse of meaningless cruelty, he picks up a stick and hurls it. The snake writhes, and is gone. The poem ends with a line that has always haunted me: 'And I have something to expiate: a pettiness.'

I wasn't deliberately cruel. Nothing in that small drama in a London garden was petty, any more than in Lawrence's Sicilian landscape. But I have something to expiate: neglect; self-absorption; and I ask myself if these things must always be the price of writing.

SUE GEE's new novel, *The Mysteries of Glass*, opens on the Welsh borders in the winter of 1860.

Coming attractions . . .

PETER OBORNE hits a six

DERVLA MURPHY recalls an Anglo-Irish past

CLARE MORRALL takes off with Biggles

JOHN KEAY puts on his apron

PENELOPE LIVELY explores the genius of William Golding

BARNABY ROGERSEN goes travelling

WILLIAM PALMER listens to Louis Armstrong

SARAH ANDERSON dives in

Bibliography

Miklos Banffy, *The Writing on the Wall: The Transylvanian Trilogy*   54

Memoirs of the Comtesse de Boigne   34

Lord Byron, *Don Juan*   44

George Ewart Evans and David Thomson, *The Leaping Hare*   7

Raymond Firth, *We the Tikopia*   49

Simon Gray, *Fat Chance; Enter a Fox; The Smoking Diaries*   12

John Griesemer, *Signal & Noise*   86

Romesh Gunesekera, *Reef*   21

Nigel Hinton, *Time Bomb*   87

Etgar Keret, *The Nimrod Flip Out*   87

Thomas Love Peacock, *Headlong Hall; Crotchet Castle*   78

Vita Sackville-West, *In Your Garden; In Your Garden Again*   74

Edwin St Aubyn, *The Patrick Melrose Trilogy*   67

Christine Sutherland, *The Princess of Siberia*   62

Alison Uttley, *The Country Child*   82

Denton Welch, *A Voice through a Cloud*   58

Patrick Wright, *Tank: The Progress of a Monstrous War Machine*   15

Taichi Yamada, *Strangers*   86

Richard Yates, *Revolutionary Road*   31

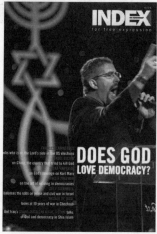

THE ROYAL SOCIETY
OF LITERATURE
LECTURES

Wednesday, 4 May: The T.S.Eliot Memorial Lecture: Don
Paterson, 'Landing Lights and Shadows'. Chair Jo Shapcott

Wednesday, 15 June: The Roy Jenkins Memorial Lecture: Jung
Chang, 'Mao: The Untold Story'. Chair Colin Thubron

The lectures take place in the Kenneth Clark Lecture Theatre, Courtauld
Institute, Somerset House, London, and begin punctually at 7 p.m.
Members of the public are welcome to attend the first lecture. The
Society suggests a contribution of £5. The second lecture is only
open to members of the Society but new members are always
welcome. For details please call 020 7845 4676.